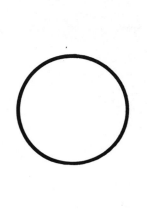

poems by

RAMON GUTHRIE

Trobar Clus
A World Too Old
Graffiti
Asbestos Phoenix
Maximum Security Ward

Ramon Guthrie
MAXIMUM SECURITY WARD

1964–1970

FARRAR, STRAUS & GIROUX
New York

Four sections of Part I—"Elegy," "Red-Headed Intern,"
"Via Crucis," and "Scene: A Bedside in the Witches'
Kitchen"—originally appeared in earlier versions in *Asbestos
Phoenix*, © 1968 by Ramon Guthrie, and are reprinted
here by permission of the publishers, Funk & Wagnalls,
New York.

The section entitled "The Making of the Bear" orig-
inally appeared in *The New Yorker*, with whose permission
it is reprinted. Grateful acknowledgments are made to *The
Carleton Miscellany*, *The Humanist*, *The Nation*, *The New
Republic*, and *The Quest*, for assignments of copyright and
permission to reprint other portions of this poem.

The author is also grateful to the Research Committee
of Dartmouth College for providing funds for the prepara-
tion of the manuscript of this book.

to
Alex, Jimmie & Steve
with love and thanks

Maximum Security Ward is a single poem composed of a number of movements which, as often as not, are fully comprehensible only by their relation to other movements and to the poem as a whole.

Contents

Even the blows of heavy surf cannot cause one sand grain to rub against another.
—Rachel Carson, *The Edge of the Sea*

Icarus, the most eccentric [of the asteroids], would hit the earth if its orbit changed by only one degree, Dr. Mazursky said.
—*The New York Times*, Oct. 18, 1967

part one

Elegy for Mélusine from the Intensive Care Ward

So name her Vivian. I, scarecrow Merlin—
our Broceliande this frantic bramble of
glass and plastic tubes and stainless steel—
could count off such illusions as I have
on a quarter of my thumbs.

>   (. . . *even a postcard of Viollet-le-Duc's*
>   *pensive chimera signed with her initial . . .*)

I penciled out a cable: FCHRISAKE COMMA
WRITE TO ME STOP YOURE LIVING AND IM DYING.
Gray lady challenged the expletive and my assurance
that it was an Ainu epithet of endearment.
I struck out everything but WRITE—cheaper
and besides I wasn't really dying
save that I couldn't breathe too well
nor feed except on intravenous dextrose.

Still stands that I am dying, Mélusine,
and have been ever since my infancy,
but the process is more measurable now.
You can tick off the months on a calendar—
eeny, meeny, miny . . . and when you get to the end . . .

>   (*Today again no word.*
>   *. . . Breton Saint Anne . . . Black Virgin*
>   *of Le Puy . . .*)

When you get to the end . . .
when you get to the end . . .
You know what *I* should like to do when I get to the end?
when I am tucked and snug and smug
with hair combed sleek for once

pants pressed   shoes shined
and tie on straight for the first time in my life?

I'd like to give one last galvanic jerk
and flip up straight and look all living beings
in the eye—all human ones, that is
(because, less lucky than are cats and cows
and bumblebees, they know that they are living)
and speak out clear: "I hate life. I who am
no longer living can speak this truth.
From my first taste of it, from the moment when
my drunken Uncle Doc dangled me by the heels
and whacked my rump, I have always hated living!"
then flop back flat into the casket with a happy
or, at least, contented or vacuous, smirk upon my face—
soundly dead for keeps this time.
That, mes amis, would be worth living long enough to see!

Every tear would dry like sizzled spit
testing a hot flatiron. The organ,
up to then simpering stately lullabies,
would burst a dozen pipes. The pallbearers
would stop dead in their tracks. (Their tracks to *where?*
Don't ask *me:* I'm only playing the lead
in this production, not directing it.)
And everybody from the preacher down
to the boy soprano would look each other in the eye
and murmur in unison:
"Why, the old bastard! Who'da thunk it of him!"
(It would be no time for grammatical niceties.)

Still . . .
bring on your Dead March with Muffled Drums
and Reversed Rifles and high-stepping young
Drum Majorettes with the minniest of Miniskirts.
Let Taps be played and Keeners keen.
Consume the Baked Meats with good appetite.
And . . .
grant me this: I *tried* to love life—
tried my damnedest but just couldn't make it.
Matter of acquired tastes you somehow can't acquire—
like some wines (Tokay, Monbazillac)
or foods (gazpacho, prune whip, lemon pie).

Fell fable of the fox that did at last
leap high enough and the grapes
definitely *were* sour.

(. . . *or an empty envelope addressed in her concise
swift runic hand.*)

Red-Headed Intern, Taking Notes

Do you been or did you never? Ha!
Speakless, can you flex your omohyoid
and whinny ninety-nine? Quick now,
can you recall your grandmother's maiden name
six times rapidly? Have you a phobia of spiders?
Only fairly large and brown ones
dropping from the ceiling?
Does this happen often, would you say?
(Nurse, clamp the necrometer when I say when.
If he passes out, tickle his nose with a burning feather
and tweak his ears counterclockwise.)
No history of zombi-ism in the immediate family?
And tularemia? No recent intercourse
with a rabbit?
      (Lash him firmly to the stretcher
      and store him in the ghast house for the night.)

Today Is Friday

Always it was going on
In the white hollow roar
you could hear it at a hundred paces if you listened closely
and a hemisphere away if you didn't listen at all
if you were paying no attention to it
fixing your mind hard on something else
        I will not hear it
        I will not hear it
        I

Screaming it inwardly so hard it seemed
your seminal vesicles must rupture with the strain
you could hear it close at hand
feel it crimping your nerve ends
your brain pan buckling in its grip
see it perform its curious rituals
as pale as ichor
limp as larvae
You could curl up with it and sleep
        Only it was not
        Only it was not
        Only it

You could taste it being fed intravenously through a
skein of tubes into your most plausible dreams
It was happening   It was going on as suavely
as if it were a rank of drop-forges
smashing diamonds to dust as fast as
they could be fed to them.

Tangible
It is a great protracted

totally transparent cube
with sides and angles
perceptibly contracting against
eyeballs and nose and mouth and skin

It is always happening
It is always going on
When it gets tired of going on
maybe it will stop

Via Crucis

Out of this   coming sidewise   slinking and
    sidling two steps forward and nine or ten
backward for fear of getting a charge of rock-salt
for a Peeping Tom . . . Gangway, lady! Gangway!
I'm doing a via crucis.
And she says, "B'jazes, it's the first time I ever seen
anybody doing one
in a hospital johnny! What are you—
a furriner or something?"
    Thou sayest it, lady. All these years
I've been wondering what I am and now I know:
    a foreigner or something. No kith, belike,
or kin of anything—at least among the higher primates—
a, biologically speaking, sport!

By what, for all its blare, must still be night,
the swift square-bottomed nurse flits sure
from bed to bed, takes blood pressures and pulses,
checks drains and bandages, switches on chest pumps.
Interns, doctors, moving in pairs,
converse in muffled nods. Approaching with a clipboard,
a small wren-faced nurse asks, "Sir,
what is your religion?" Religion?
"I have to ask you just in case." None.
She marks the X at Protestant.

MR. GOLDBLATT: STAFF NURSE (white letters on
blue plastic badge) buzzing like an officious
bottlefly doing an imitation of Schnozzle Durante,
struts in by what, if they would give me back my watch,
must now be morning. There are no windows though

to judge that by, only these cones of light
trained on our eyelids . . . high iron grills
fencing in each of the nearly touching beds
constantly being (one man dying or making guggling
sounds of death, another in new-bloodied bandages
arriving) trundled in or out.

"HELLO, OL' SPORT! How you doin', ol' sport?
Come on, ol' sport, roll over so I can insert . . .
Look here, ol' sport, you just always do
just like I tell you and we'll get along fine."

Maximum Security Ward. Sure, I know . . .
Intensive Care Ward, but none the less,
straight out of Jacques Callot by Hogarth.
"What time they bring him in here? 2 a.m.?"

No, so to speak, white corpuscles. Your guess
why not, as good as mine: all I know
is chattering teeth and thirst.

"Look here, ol' sport,
I give you ginger ale a while ago.
You'da been thirsty, you'da drunk it
instead of yammerin' for water now.
You don't like ginger ale, it ain't my fault.
I'm busy now, I got my records to keep up."

MR. GOLDBLATT, you cloacal breathed, glad-handing ghoul,
if ever I get my white
corpuscles out of hock

and temperature down enough to take it orally,
I'm going to vault that side rail and ram
those outsized, clicking dentures down your throat,
God be my witness. SELAH.

Cadenza

"My name is Marsyas,"
                    says ram
says ram to Abraham
caught in the thicket by the horns,
"My name is Marsyas."
Name of father? "None.
Look, I know an altar when I see one."
Name of mother? Come on, name of mother?
"All right. Hagar.
And don't make believe you never heard of her."

The square-bottomed nurse's night is over.
She is about to leave. She wipes
sweat from her forehead
and pushes her hair back under her cap.
She stops, turns back. "You comf'table? You don't look it.
You want I should see if I could do
sumpen about those pillows before I go?"

Scene: A Bedside
in the Witches' Kitchen

DOCTOR *to his retinue of interns and residents:*
Obvious ptoritus of the drabia.
Although the prizzle presents no sign of rabies,
note this pang in the upper diaphrosis.
When kicked there hard enough, the patient utters,
"Yoof!" and curls up like a cutworm.
I prescribe bedcheck every hour on the hour
with intensive catalepsis. (*Exeunt.*)

PATIENT *to Nurse:*
My name is Marsyas, a stranger here.
　　　　　　　How to explain?
Sprächen zoo something? anything? Aard-vark? Gnu?
you look well-meaning. If I made noises in my phlarynx
and shaped them with my phtongue, would they have
snignifigance to you? Or would they merely
confuse us further? Let's go about it anagogically.
Close your ears. Go twine your sphygmomanometer
about some other patient or administer him his hem-
　　lock,
while I supplicate.

　　　　　　Today is Friday.

Gamut of goddesses, Gaia, Latona, Frigg whose day it is,
cat-flanked Ishtar with the up-turned palms,
Rosmertha of the Gauls, with grief-gouged eyes
and rough-hewn cleft—
　　　　　sister, mother, mistress of the dead,
mare-shaped Epona, you, Venus of Lespugue
in mammoth tusk, majestic at scarce a handsbreadth tall,

though not quite small enough to put into a matchbox
and walk the streets of Montparnasse with in your pocket . . .

Gamut of goddesses,
in your spare moments intercede for me . . .
    (Breath comes scant now,
     but by chance you may have heard,
       my name is Marsyas) . . .
intercede for me. Let me be never born.
Let my ghost wander in brambled upland meadows.
Drizzle in evening streets, may she at times recall
our walking there, arms pressed to ribs together.

Mélusine!

Montparnasse . . .

Montparnasse
that I shall never see again, the Montparnasse
of Joyce and Pound, Stein, Stella Bowen,
little Zadkine, Giacometti . . . all gone in any case,
and would I might have died, been buried there.

[GIACOMETTI]

". . . impression that art would come easy to me . . .
getting what I wanted . . . now, 50 years later . . .
At 13 I did a head of Diego and have done
nothing better since . . . Am no closer.
Tintoretto effaced by the Giottos of Padua
blotted out in turn by Cimabue . . .
Sculpture anti-form—*of*, not *in*, space
. . . rather see a bird flying in the sky
than any masterpiece of art . . ."

A fixture in the quarter with his furrowed face
from the first day he came there
to study with Bourdelle.
       Giacometti standing in the dank, littered shed
that was his atelier, lighting one Gauloise from
the short stub of another, standing because
there was no place to sit, explained
a great many things, such as carrying about
his work of four whole years in half-a-dozen
matchboxes scattered through his pockets and working
for years with the same model without ever
speaking to her—explained many things by saying,
"La vie n'est qu'un suicide passif."
That's one way of looking at it; it takes longer
than holding your head in a gas oven

or jumping off the Pont Neuf some darkish night,
but just as effective. He proved it: lung cancer, 1966.

Gamut of goddesses, intercede (presumably with
yourselves) for me.
                    Today is Friday . . .
                                        vendredi . . .

Venus of flesh . . .
            (Landing at Naples:
        Colonel Bill's curly-headed
        unpanted daughter panting for the plane.)
Au fond perhaps   of limited lascivity . . .
Les yeux cernés, tendres mais sans la moindre tendresse.

"Side by Side"

Side by side   but scant sharing
Little of fellowship here   Some of us for dying
    Some for living   Some half a mind each way.

    Should I have willed my corneas?
    My old but still staunch heart?
    my cadaver *in toto?* Medical schools will pay
    good money in advance for a second-hand cadaver.

        No! not to have my brine-shriveled scrotum
    bandied about, my epididymis unraveled, measured by
    some embryo Bovary.

No fellowship . . . How the dying wince
            from the living's shadows!
How the living fear the kinship of the dead!
I do not know which side I'm on—
the dyings' or the livings' (that small minority,
of us though not aware of it)
No, on the whole, I am on the side of the dead once they
    have
achieved atonement with the earth
and of the living who do not want
even in their secret hearts to die.

    "I don' wanna by-nit up me arsole
    I don' wan' me bollicks shot awy-y-y
    I wanna go to Blighty
    To dear ol' blinkin' Blighty
    An' there I wanna fook meself awy-y-y."

Singing this or something similar with gusto
as they trudged up into the lines at 2nd Mons,
humming it under their breaths, wriggling on hips and elbows
across no-man's-land between the bursts of starshells.

"Leaned on the trigger and let the blighter 'ave
a bellyful just as 'e was abaht
to let *me* 'ave a 'titer-marsher—
narsty fings them 'titer-marshers.
Don't harf mike a mess of yer, they don't."

I wanna go to Blighty
To dear ol' blinkin' Blighty
An' there I wanna . . .

"Got it proper, ol' Robby did. Real cushy.
Though Ah donno's Ah'd want it that bad—
as soon they didn't ship me home. Just
patch me up an' shove me back into the trenches.
Don't need 'em none for fightin'.
Maybe 'appier without 'em anywhere, but still an' all . . .
Goin' down from the dressin' station,
all bandaged so you couldn't reely tell,
wot with all that dope shot into 'im,
but kinder guessin', he says, 'Sy, mitey,
'ow's for the loan of your Enfield for a sec—
just to kinder finish up the job?' "

A coward dies a thousand deaths.
Rate me no coward then: 990-some yet to go.

Just seven as I make it, three times with pneumonia
(out of ten in all). Once Naples to Algiers
flying the deck—that hungry waterspout.
The kiefed-up sidi with the razor in the tram.
Once coming out of anesthesia with
an oxygen mask and much undue ado.
Then this last time, so close they thought it best
to take the copyright in my wife's name.

     Don't count
that afternoon at Flirey: handful of us standing around
watching a chess game under an oak
and desultory one-o-fives looping overhead
and landing in the beet fields half a mile beyond . . .
If you hear it, it is not for *you.* Look hard
and you could even see them, bumbling lumps
with the muzzle velocity of an oxcart.
The zouave had just castled and announced,
"Echec au roi."
Wordless, triggered by a sudden hunch, we flowed
down into the dugout.
The zouave—he owned the game—it seems reached back
to snatch the white queen, his *porte-bonheur.*
We heard one WHUNGPH, waited a moment to see
if there were more to come, decided not,
emerged in time to see the *brancardiers*
loading the zouave's remains.
As Louis told the tale, his hand still clutched
the lucky queen and the *obus* had landed
in the exact center of the chessboard—
accurate within perhaps ten paces.

I do not count that afternoon nor would
if the fuse itself had struck
square on my cranial suture, death no more
real for me than for the fool squirrel
racing to throw a body block
on an oncoming truck.

  Too young to think that we could ever die.

The Cube as a Wilted Prism

The
walls now extend   recede to everywhere.
The ceiling, though still low, outcrops the stratosphere.
The drop-forge rank
chumbles and crunks more diamonds faster into dust
and grids space with crisscross false horizons.
Distance presses, cramps, distends.

This cube
has 6 faces, 12 edges, 24 angles
each more fluctuating pinched and forced a-spread
than all the others. Space. Sculpture not *in*
but *of* Space. Eroding Space. Ripples,
billows, bellies out to burst,
yet, contracting, shrinks tight within, upon itself—
soundless explosion squeezed to utmost condensation.

    (I *know*—like trying to explain
    the concept and sensation of
    wetness to a, say, intelligent and
    articulate fish, *piscis sapiens*—
    or darkness to a mole.)

. . . become a fast-expanding, prismic,
limp though hard, Brobdingnagian HERE including THERE,
devoid of direction.
You might scream now if you so wished:
sound cannot travel in such vast whiteness.

Equation with death—liquescent crystal Death,
as dry, invisible as pure

self-consuming flame,
becomes inevitable.

The cross-hair sight of Never and Now
is set in all zeniths, on all horizons.
It is stamped with hot wire
on my breastbone.

Polar Bear

That time coming out from under
sodium pentathol my first words were,
"I dreamt I was a polar bear
that couldn't write poetry."
Literally but to unhearing ears.

 Adrift upon that slab of floe
 under a slate sky
 his conic white
 snout swaying in unison
 with words that never came.

The small deft nurse who held
the glass tube to my lips
said, "Sip slowly,
a little at a time. Don't raise your head."

I, not yet aware that words were speech,
informed her,
"You are quite lovely
with your copper hair.
You look like something that was turned
     into a flower
before it was a girl again . . . I can't explain."

Later she came back and asked
how I was feeling. "Not bad," I lied,
the anesthesia now wearing thin.
She laid her hand against my face.
"Still you had better have this though."
An easy needle slipped into my shoulder.

A polar bear who could not . . .
Rocking his baffled muzzle to and fro
groping for the tempo of a world
empty of both sense and sound.

I wondered—whatever was in the needle
taking now effect—what had become of him
and brooded over not trying to find a way to help him,
staying at least to share
the anguish of his white bewilderment.

The Archangel Michael,
or a reasonable facsimile thereof,
holds a press conference:

". . . Embarked upon a Holy Crusade whose
holy purpose . . . on this there is no general accord."
[Subdued applause.] As Mr. Eisenhower has explained,
'the natives were tired of *any* form
of overlordship . . . wanted their independence'
and having won it, took it into their thick peasant heads
to resent the mercenaries whom we sent
to liberate them from it—
instead of turning the other cheek to be kicked.

"Holy—as I was saying—Crusade.
What them native races need is a little humility,
start off by getting right down on their knees
and praying the good Lord to give it to them.
What you mean—the Buddhists *have* no god?
Don't they worship idols or something
like everybody else? Maybe that's right where
the whole trouble lies!"

    ". . . *All because we do not car-ry*
     Everything to God in prayer."

"Yessiree! You just try that next time
and see if everything won't come out right.
That way, about the only trouble that a fellow
can have is getting callouses on his knees!"

ME, MEL TROTTER, LORD,
You remember? You found me lying filthy drunk
in a gutter, Lord, so hog-dirty no human being
would have wanted to soil his hands by touching me.

But You did, Lord.
You picked me up and washed me in Your own Son's blood
and sent me forth to preach Your word throughout
the length and breadth of this whole land.
What did I ever do to deserve it, Lord?
Nothing, O Lord. Nothing.
All I deserved was hell-fire, but You had mercy on me.
You and Your Son. You sent me here tonight, Lord,
to pass Your holy Word on to these boys.
They too are sinners, Lord, but that won't keep You
from entering right into their hearts and making them
clean and pure   Let us now sing together:

> *Just as I am without one plea*
> *But that Thy blood was shed for me*
> *And that Thou bidst me come to Thee-ee,*
> *O Lamb of God, I come, I come.*

Will you come to Jesus? Will you let
Jesus come into your heart? Will *you?* Will *you?*
Hold up your hands, brothers, if you will.
Will you give yourself to Christ? Hold up your hand . . .
I see you, brother . . . I see you, brother . . . I see you.
And what about *you*, brother? Are you too *brave* to come
to Jesus? Too sure that you can face temptation all alone?
So certain that you can lick the Devil singlehanded
that you don't *want* Jesus on your side? We're waiting,
brother. We're praying for you.

> *Just as I am and waiting not*
> *To rid my soul of one dark blot*

To thee, whose blood can cleanse each spot,
O Lamb of God, I come, I come.

AN USHER (*whispering loudly. He is also co-captain of the*
    football team):
Come on, guy. Put up your hand
We want to make this school 100% for Jesus Christ.
Put it up. Do you want him to keep us here all night?

Holy, holy, holy . . .

The press conference ends when the sergeants-at-arms,
preceded by a huge bass drum, march in singing,
"Onward Christian soldiers, marching as to war,"
and carrying pikes on which heathen heads with
wispy beards are impaled.

Inventory

     Hmm, let's see now . . .
On the left we have what is left
On the right is what is right
It is that simple . . .
   Faith, hope and clarity . . .
I knew a girl named Faith once,
on shipboard and in both senses

     To be a model patient you lie on your back,
     screen your eyes with the back of your wrist
     against the glaring cone of light
     and wait the chance to pour unnoticed
     the ginger ale into the urinal—
     bringing variety into the life
     of some laboratory technician.

Gamut of goddesses . . . with a few gods thrown in . . .
Diana of Ephesus with her cluster
of breasts, looking like something dreamt
of a Saturday night by a perverse computer
primed with LSD . . .
Priapic Marsyas or Silenus as shown
on a black-figured vase ("young man from Nantucket")
tootling his heart out
on upraised double flute . . .

Check again, placing the patient this time
on a sphere spinning on its own axis at
1000 miles an hour and in its orbit at
66,000 mph. And now?
               Through dizzy eyes:

On the left is nothing left
On the right nothing is right.

I have lived. Listen to that!
Say it again, ol' sport. *I have lived.*
       Of all the witless things to say,
I give you this!

Gamut of goddesses, Nerthus, Frigg (Friday's girl),
Rosmertha and You
the veiled and nameless one, bless me.
Still the blood-flow in my veins,
numb fingers' touch, quell thought and feeling
in my brain.
       For now,
surveying that churned wake, I know
that by some slip or quirk,
I have led a stranger's life, known with his mind,
spoken with his tongue, kissed with his lips,
worshipped or denied his gods . . .
  (Mix-up in cloak-room checks—
      sole-print perhaps)
and now must die this death of his for him.

The Flute

MARSYAS: (*He takes his flute and seems about to play it,
thinks better of it and slips it back into the pocket of his
bathrobe. He resumes his meditation.*)

'A stranger's life?' I said. *Many* strangers.
Known with their minds . . . their eyes . . . their lips . . .
Worshipped their gods . . . heard with their ears?
Felt, have I, with their hearts—a moment mine?

That appeal—in Mozart now, I mean, the string quintet.
Adagio. Muted—you can't mute a flute.
Two notes legato: *sol fa.* A silence.
    Two notes: *do si.* A pause buoyed up and weighted
        with grief too pure to· be grief—
or any other feeling *I* could ever know,
and then that linked descending run . . .
        The ache and wonder!
And *simple.* Two notes. A rest. Two more notes,
higher this time—appealing, questioning, calling out—
            to what?
A rest. And then that flow.
That's all that I remember clearly of it.
        (*He takes the flute again, looks at it dubiously, puts it to
    his lips and plays:*

*He listens for a moment, takes the flute between his hands,
breaks it in two and drops the pieces to the floor. The night
nurse picks them up and hands them to him. Without
looking at her, he carefully puts them back into his pocket.*)

Icarus Agonistes

A damsel with a clip-board in an Intensive Care Ward
once I saw
in a white uniform and she was asking,
"Sir, what is your religion?" with a pencil poised
to check it off. I should have said Black Muslim,
but I didn't think of it until a week later.

> . . . one straggling and on the whole
> incurious sheep that happens
> to be facing the other way from
> the rest of the flock seems to have heard the splash
> and paused an instant in its cropping . . .
> the shepherd gawking but in the diametrically
> wrong direction.

> "Come on, ol' sport . . . ol' sport."

Stand on a haystack and flap your arms.
You see, you almost *did* fly! Someday
try it from the corncrib roof. Or, Joshua—
hold up your arm and, as watching your shadow
you can clearly see, stop the sun for a split second.

> C'est pourtant vrai: Mourir c'est partir un peu.
> (Sure, I know how it *should* go. If I don't think
> hard enough about it, I know how almost *ev-*
> *erything* should go. The trouble is
> sometimes I think, and I'm not good at it.
> Right now I think I hear a tinkling sound
> above all other racket. And *mourir* is
> *partir* quite a lot.)

I see a cart.
Please, Mr. Good Humor Man, you with the starched
white clothes! (I see the cart and hear the jingle.)
Would any of your tranquilizers lay
the ghosts of Twink and Stella? Norman Fitts?
Please, Mister Good Humor Man, You with the long white
   beard
and cart and bell. You, Mister Summertime Saint Nick,
I have died my allotted thousand deaths
and served my time in hell
after each one of them.
                  The bell, please. The bell . . .
You may not have noticed it, but I've been out on my feet
since the first round. Really *out,*
slobbering, glassy-eyed, rubber-legged,
hooking my chin on something's shoulder and hanging on
to hear the bell

     The winnuh
                and still champeen
   is whatever
           I got myself overmatched with
      from the start.

(From somewhere a very old and tired tape
    is heard faintly urging:
      "Fight your *left,* baby! Fight your *left!*
Back him up, baby! Back him up!
Fight your left! F'get yuh got a right! Don't think,
just fight your left!"
              BONG.

"Listen, baby. Can yuh hear me? Yuh still got him cold
if yuh don't go right-hand crazy. Fight your left.
Don't think. F'get yuh *got* a brain."
    BONG.
"Awright, baby. We get him nex' time maybe.
Him or somebody else.
      Plenty times already
you been flattened almost as bad as this.")

Fiercer Than Evening Wolves . . .

Lying here in truth more disgruntled
than in any great discomfort, shaped to this
tapered wedge of cosmos, wondering
if there would be relief in having a God to hate . . .
I've tried it—believing there was one, that is.
"Everything," says Blake, "possible to be believed
is an image of the truth." Whether a God's being
is "possible to be believed" by me
I shall probably die without discovering.

To while the night away, try now imagining
for symbol's sake a man bigger than
any professional basketball or football player.
Something to the scale of the Rhodes Colossus
or the Pharaohs of Abu-Simbel. Bearded. Naked
or in a sort of off-the-shoulder toga? Both.
And with a clutch of writhing thunderbolts.
Zeus, Thor, Quetzalcoatl all in one.
Endow him with omnipotence, omniscience, omnipresence . . .
All to no end.

    I lie here remembering, half-envying
my truly pious mother, who did believe—
totally, always, absolutely and without
shading or limitation   and died
selecting, as she hoped,
the most telling of blasphemies,
mastered her mangled speech to utter it precisely,
enunciated, "God is a cunt," straining to say
the word for the first time in her life,
sure that He was hearing her,

that she was in His hands
and soon would stand defenseless
in His presence.

"What," the red-headed intern asks, "did your father die of?"
Another's suicide. Illuminating gas. He broke down
the door of the hotel room. The blast
broke windows blocks away.
"And your mother? Please, no accidents."
This was no accident. Of that we can be sure.
Swallowing a massive dose of potassium chlorate—
no, not the cyanide she'd begged me for—
in the charity ward of the New Haven Hospital.
The story, both longer and shorter than it should have been,
boils down mostly to arithmetic? How is
your arithmetic, doctor?

THE ARITHMETIC LESSON
    If one room's rent with cooking privileges came
    to $7 a week, and 60 times 20 cents an hour
    is $12 and you had to put a quarter in
    the gas meter from time to time and shoes
    and clothes wore out or got outgrown and on
    days when you were working on the other side of town
    you had to take the trolley,
    how did you eat and feed your young?
    Simple. By taking in sewing to do at home
    nights and Sundays. Quod erat demonstrandum.

        Evenings between
        cooking and doing the housework and getting back

to sewing, she would read the Bible to me.
Especially the Old Testament. I liked that best—
even Jeremiah and Habakkuk . . . *Their horses swifter*
    than leopards and fiercer than evening
        wolves . . .
and Ezekiel with his cherubim on beryl monocycles.
She skipped the parts about Dinah's boy-friend
getting circumcised and the two Tamars
and the Lord making the Israelites
hamstring the horses and rip up
the bellies of pregnant ladies.
Yes, the Lord God fared very well by Her—
better than She did by him, by far.

In her mid-forties when successive strokes
twisted her mouth awry, mangled her speech,
paralyzed the right side of her body,
there were, each with its acute
eternity enhanced by helplessness,
some 86 thousand seconds in a day.
"She's young," the trim-cut doctor jibed. "May well
live on like this another twenty years."
Roughly 600 million seconds, each more
desperate than the last.
        Would you let
a half-crushed spider live a millionth part as long?
        ". . . fiercer than evening wolves . . ."
    Does that answer your question, doctor?
    Nothing hereditary, I should say.

The Oracles

> **HAPPEN**
> **OR DO NOT HAPPEN**
> **HAS OR HAS NOT HAPPENED**
> **WILL OR WILL NOT HAPPEN**

gouged on a crude lead slab set into
the most remote blind gut of the cavern.
Mephitic vapors will extinguish torches.
It can be deciphered only by touch.

Hugging her breasts, the Pythoness rocks in anguish.
Deep in her trance, she sees with open eyes
all that has been and is about to be.
Hugs her breasts, rocks to and fro and moans.
She wakes. Juice of freshly pressed nepenthes
dribbles from her slack mouth.
The wail becomes a whimper, a gape, a blank
foolish, rather evil, smile.
                            She knows
and cannot undo knowing
        nor forget she knows.
            Her eyeteeth are small fangs.

She cannot weep or pray:
all that has ever happened
        all that is to happen
she knows.

There Are Those

Qui bien ce croit, peu ne merit
Gens mors estre faiz petiz dieux
François Villon

There are those—with mine own eyes I've seen them,
heard them with my own ears—
who still contrive to believe in heaven,
locus undisclosed, though rather up than down.
(Quoting sound authority, "All men will arise
with the same bodies they have now." Is that
something to feel good about?)

Alice B. Toklas, passing from Jew to atheist to
Roman Catholic, on being baptized, asked,
"Does this mean I'll see Gertrude when I die?"

Our belovèd Walshes—Paddy and Mim!
Come straight from Dublin to Arizona, himself
having but half a lung (T.B. arrested when we met them).
The warmth and wit of them. The good foolish
games that we concocted. The good talk.
The punning Latin sonnets to wish us happy birthdays.

    "Look, Paddy, nothing could ever make me believe
in that heaven of yours."
        "Of God's, more strictly speaking . . .
And all the luckier for you. Think of your surprise
when you'll be waking up and saying, 'I still don't believe
in all this heaven stuff!' and God just grinning,
'Nor do you have to, man. Not if not believing
makes you any happier. We aim to please.' "
    "But if there were a heaven, what makes you think
I'd ever get there?"
        "Because it wouldn't *be* a heaven
for Mim and me unless you were." And Mim,

though apt to leave theology to Paddy, joined in,
"That's God's own truth—it wouldn't be, you know.
But you'll be there all right. We being older,
we're like to get there first. You'll find us waiting."

Paddy . . . Mim . . .
I hadn't seen you all these forty years.
Two Christmases ago we didn't get
our usual letter from you.
Later a stranger wrote that you had died
a week apart, leaving word that you had always missed us
and never known anyone you'd been fonder of . . .
    Paddy . . . Mim . . .

Paddy was a man—a good man but still
        only a man.
If I know Mim, it would take a lot more
than there not *being* any heaven
to keep her from going there, if only to make sure
that Paddy had all he'd ever need to make him happy—
Not but what she trusted God . . .
                but still . . .

The Prayers

To M. C.

Prayers, I age 8 asked, do they get answered?
The reply was patient but categoric.
Then why not, instead of asking for just enough
to make some payment on back rent, pray big—
ask for a hundred or a billion dollars
and never have to bother Him again?

     Interrogatory prayer, whom are you asking what?
"I'm asking the dead what death is like and the living
what it is like to live. I am asking this housefly,
sealed somehow between panes, perhaps hatched there,
buzzing its life away against impenetrable light,
whether it would rather be let out into
the foreign air, stay where it is, or be
let in and whacked by a flyswatter."

     Look, fly. I won't hurt you. I only want to scare you out.
Don't waste your life penned up in here
where there isn't any future for you.
Don't you want to copulate and eat and see
           something of the world?
I'm unfastening the storm window for you.
Get the hell outdoors where you were meant to be.
Nothing was ever meant to live in houses.
Doesn't it give you claustrophobia? It does me.
Even *cimex lectularius*, more familiarly known as bedbug,
's natural habitat is outdoors under the bark of trees.
In the beginning *was* no bed (see
Genesis 1:1–2, St. John 1:1, and Faust's
'Im Aufang war die Tat'—Deed, indeed!)
Adam begot Cain, Cain begot Enoch . . . Lamech begot

Jubal, father of all flute *and* harp players.
And Abraham upon Hagar, his maidservant, begot
Ishmael whose 'hand will be against every man,'
—all at least 34 hundred years before
the first inner-spring mattress was invented.

Gamut of goddesses, Eastre,
Black Virgin of Le Puy,
Louise Michel, *la vierge rouge,*
born to a maidservant by the master's son . . .
last stand of the Commune, surrounded, hopelessly out-armed,
    outnumbered,
in the Montmartre cemetery—
about 30,000 murdered out of hand,
the survivors, she miraculously among them,
deported half-a-world away to New Caledonia.
Came back to preach LIBERTY through France
unto the day she died.

"My name is Marsyas,"
        says ram to Abraham.
"I play the flute. Keep your rabbinical hands off me.
I know an altar when I see one.
And no good ever came of one yet.
By the way, where is your *real* firstborn,
the one you drove into the desert?"

Hey,
interrogatory prayer! I'm not done with you yet.
Whom else do you ask what else of?
"I ask all sorts of things all sorts of questions.

I am asking questions of the walls and ceiling,
of the cocoon of bandages in a coma beside me.
I am asking questions of the ground and sky
of places I shall never see again, asking our belovèd
Mim and Paddy Walsh if there really is
a heaven (they owe me a jug of corn whiskey if there isn't)
and how they like it there.
I am asking the handsome Black Muslim masseuse
on 88th Street, who told me, 'I jes' *love* po'try!'
whether she ever spreads her fine, strong,
horse-chestnut-textured legs to Allah.
I am asking questions of skin and nerves and glands,
tits and tummies. I am asking lips
how they first learned to suck, to shape first words.
Here I am, not too short of being dead
and with no idea of what one actually *does*
to perform such simple acts as swallowing and sneezing,
let alone ejaculating or falling asleep."

> (*You, Ishmael, take Marsyas, to be your blood-
> brother. Make your X there in the lower corner
> and don't read the fine print too carefully.*)

Exploratory prayer, addressed to whom?
what are you asking It or Her or Him
to say or do? What language, spoken by what
paralyzed or petrified tongue, are you uttered in?

Formed not of dust but quicksand.
Lie prostrate in the muck, face buried deep in it,
and try

for breath to
propitiate
Him, Her, or It
with gasping mad doxologies and screamed hosannahs.
      . . . and yet
. . . and yet
      . . . ram caught by the horns
     in a thicket. We find the theme
        in gold and lapis lazuli at Ur of the Chaldees.
   Poor bloody Marsyas—teach him to steer clear
         of angels
("A little lower than the angels" . . . ,
Some of whom
   could walk under a snake's ass
with high hats on . . . unquote the sergeant
   who had served in the calvary
   with Captain Black-Jack Perishing
   christianizing them Moros in the Philippines)
and yet
      . . . And yet . . .

"Loin de Moi . . ."
Robert Desnos

Far from me
light shattering copper balls across
   the stubbled hillsides in October
seeing fox pounce daintily on crickets,
standing on a boulder acknowledging
the reverent ranks of mullein,
flapping my wings and disclaiming, "No.
I am not God! I am not God! . . . Only
one of his archangels, Michael for choice,
excepting on such days as I fill in
for Israfel or Orpheus."
Far from me godhood
and the creaking crazy stars doing
their cumbersome quadrilles to patchwork patterns
concocted here on earth: Bootes the Herdsman,
Lyra and the ram Aries.
Far from me vermeil diadem, globe and scepter,
loving-cups for taking Beelzebub in straight sets
or scoring eagles over Satan. Far from me be
all honors, loves and worships except a few
passing and very momentary idolatries.
Far from me in this moment
everything that lived and now is dead,
everything that lives and soon will die,
everything I loved that now is gone.
You who were absent from the place of the Skull,
let my self itself be far from me.
Far from me. Far from me. There is no return from here
to color, clarity, or form. Sound aplenty
but not a thud or scrape or drone to shape to any harmony.
There is a stocky, squat, somebody's sister—

somebody's daughter, at any rate—with swollen ankles,
blouse like saddlebags. Night built up in layers
of chlorine and last year's puke and piss.
If I should beat my head against the bars,
they would put it down to delirium.

Dawn . . . dear Mr. white-jacketed God, please send dawn.
Dawn. I couldn't see it here
but maybe catch a whiff of it.
I am stretched out here dreading dawn as if it were
a more malignant form of night.
(I must not let myself guess that.)
I am lying here trying to remember how to laugh
against the chance
of anything to laugh for   ever again occurring.
I am lying here not screaming—as good a pastime
as any. I am lying here trying to refrain
from trying to remember anything.
I am lying here stifling in the rutty goat smell
of MR. GOLDBLATT:STAFF NURSE and death.

Mélusine!
("I cannot write," she said. "For me a letter
is artifice that only enhances distance and
aggravates the ache of separation." Clasping my hand
beneath a café table at Montparnasse.)

I am lying here trying not to see these bars,
not to envy everyone who died with pants on—
those, for instance, who went down in flames at La Chaussée.
Lying here wondering what I am doing here at all.

No. I don't mean here in this death house.
I mean HERE where MR. GOLDBLATTS are.
I mean here in these United States— "Breathes there
                    a man with soul so dead . . . ?" Yes, *I* do—
though for how long I cannot say.
I mean this world, for that matter, this human world.

(I never asked to be human. I don't and never did
opt to be human. Given any choice, I should rather
have been begotten by a dog-fox on a vixen
or an alley tom on a good mouser or—
though that may be too much to wish—
not to have been begotten at all. Quarter of a billion
spermatozoa scatter-sprayed, one gets its random target,
to the ultimate consternation of all concerned.

I never wanted to be *me*, in this at least
I found, it seems, fulfillment. (Listen carefully, cat,
cock your head on one side and wrap your tail
about your paws. You stand as good a chance
of understanding this as any.) I cannot think
of anyone less me than I am. There should be
surcease in that. Everybody—the red-headed intern,
the old man making death-sounds in the corner crib,
the low-slung nurse winding up her nightly stint . . .
Even the CHIEF HEAD IMPERIAL MR GOLDBALLS: STAFF NURSE
is more like me than I am.

. . . sizzle out like crackerbarrelers' spit
on the potbellied stove . . . sizzled out . . .
like other lives . . . What kind of a life is that,

a life like other lives, I ask you?
                                    No,
I don't ask anybody anything. Not even what
time it is. Not even anything. Just as I wouldn't—
after the Sopwith fell apart and bent
the machine-gun yoke across my forehead
and Raz came down a few days later
to see me at the hospital—I wouldn't ask the bastard
who he was. Having trouble enough recalling
just the fringes of who *I* was.

So now, at what by my watch, if they would give it back to
    me,
must be about seven-thirty,
I will not ask anything of any so-and-soing body
in the world . . .
                        Certainly
never to be human . . . The HUMAN RACE!
No, not even for the laughs. The race of
napalm Santa Clauses!
Sheep herded by glib lies that greed concocts,
he-harpies safely out of sight and sound
cheerily showering some thousand tons of bombs
on the innocent helpless to strike back,
pointless despoilers and defilers of what
might elsewise be a fairly pleasant world.

AND YET . . .

Boul' Miche, May 1968

Last night's tear gas still stinging in the air.
Paving blocks still in piles. Girl huddled on the
sidewalk, scalp bleeding, arms covering her face
against the troopers' boots and bludgeons. This
boy not even a spectator   a passer-by on his way
home in the nearby Rue Gay-Lussac. His rush took
the C.R.S. sergeant by surprise   sent him reeling
up against the grill. Wilting beneath the thuds,
the boy   eighteen or so   managed to throw himself across
the girl.
At the *commissariat* revived enough for questioning,
he could only say, "On est français, quoi!"
Not only had never seen the girl before   was not a
student nor even a sympathizer. On the whole against
the lot of them for burning cars and felling all those
trees for barricades   But when cops took to clubbing
girls for fun . . .
They had a police surgeon stitch his head, locked him up
for the night and on his mother's pleading sent him
home.
The concussion and double vision were gone in a month
or so and he went back to the accountant's office where
he worked.
The episode cost the boy his employer's confidence.
He was skipped over for promotion and given to understand
that there was no room for reds in the business.

(Thunderclaps are heard.
Off Scylla a waterspout scours seashells
from the seabed and hurls them above the clouds.
The young English pilot tugs the wheel
and hauls the yoke into his gut.)

part two

Don't and Never Did

". . . don't and never did
opt to be human. Given any choice, would rather
have been begotten by a dog-fox on a vixen
or an alley tom on a good mouser . . ."

   Retract? No,
not retract, but put it this way.
You've got to be something—right? Now Zeus—
everyone knows Zeus, the papa of the gods?
He has everything, all the advantages, including being
     purely mythical.
Maketh like a swan and screweth Leda,
maketh like a bull and slips it to Europa—
and keeps his godhead dignity throughout.
Smote the Titans and everybody else
he felt like smiting. Yahweh, Dagon,
Baal, Wodin, Shiva, Moloch,
weren't in the same league with him.
Lick his weight in wildcats without half trying.
Ares the war god, Apollo who flayed Marsyas,
Hermes, were his sons, Aphrodite,
Athena, Artemis among his daughters.

All right, could I be Zeus, I still would choose
rather to be human, to stand beside
certain humans, even from afar. Or if,
impervious as was never any god,
I could be an ultimate grain of sand,
my choice would stay the same.
      I say this knowing
that soon in some brash, noisome realm

where Pluto-Goldblatts reign, and weary, hurrying,
taut or soggy nurses are all there are
in line of houris, I shall die—
last installment on the price of being man.

Nobody will administer extreme,
or any other kind of, unction to me,
no Greuze depict my touching deathbed scene.

Thou ministering vampire, spade-chinned
oakum-wigged Sairey Gamp of the cobalt age
(no, I will not believe
this horny-knuckled, steel-rimmed hagfish hath
what I shall never touch again or see . . . God
let it not be so!) aroint thee.
Let me hold the glass, old spinster spider;
I know your ways. Uncup your claw
from under my occiput.
Aroint! I said. Scuttle back crabwise
into that foul funnel of your web,
drawing that musty effluvium of yours behind you.
Yes, I still want a drink but not that badly.
Better men than ever I was have died of thirst.

Now, shorn of upper-case and P-for-poor,
"The old bastard in 10-B's been trundled to the morgue.
A nice kid with a slightly fractured whatzis
he got skiing is taking over his bed."

Don't shave and rouge and powder me,
slick down my hair. Don't make me look presentable,

which I never did except young and naked
or all decked out in battle dress with all the ribbons.
Let me look dead and tired and old,
and no one look on me.

Icarus to Eve

Madam, I'm Adam
madA m'I, madaM
Madam, I'm Icarus, your son.
The one who flew too near the sun. Remember? No?

The elder Brueghel sees and sums it all:
not even a ripple in the bright small waves.
Steered by the title, the eye looks twice to find
the limp, unwieldy, disappearing legs.
(The headlong carcass outdistanced breath and sense:
sheer velocity makes instant anesthesia.)
Filling the foreground, the plowman goes about
finishing his chore. The contoured furrows and
horse's humble rump spell order and patience.
A man is fishing from the bank. Beyond,
a gawking shepherd seems to let his flock
tend *him*. A dog of sorts sits at his feet.
Nearby a ship, a fresh wind in her sails,
heads down the estuary. Sailors are on deck
and in the rigging. In this tight cosmos, nothing
notes the splash—except perhaps a rod or so away
one straggling sheep that seems to lift its muzzle
a moment from its grazing. A spring day is ending.
A pale smudged sun is setting in the sea.
Madam, I am Icarus, your son.
Wax melted when I flew too near . . . Remember?
No? There's no wonder. I have so many siblings
that the only wonder is that even
an absent-minded sheep should note our fall.

(Without us, legs would still be fins.
"Johnny! Don't you go too near that land.
You want to get all dry!")

This Stealth

This stealth surrounding dying . . .
            reject from a conveyor bed . . .
                    A nod . . . a nod . . .
Checking watch
MR GOLDBLATT makes an annotation

            Leaving more room
until another bed . . .

        The Magdalenian man, who graved and painted
        those bulls and charging bison on cave walls,
        tread on the fossilized remains
        of long extinct Solutreans, whose kitchen middens
        had piled up on dust or fossil forms
        of Aurignacians, one of whom had shaped
        the ivory mother goddess of Lespugue.
        Before that were Mousterians, who shaped their flints
        to fit a solid fist, Acheulians, Chellians,
        men of Neanderthal.
            At what point something ceased
        being whatever it was and became
                human—
        first animal aware
        of death—not even the most assiduous
        study of a stray molar here and there
        will let us say.
Human I never would have chosen to be,
yet grant the poor bastard this: his lust, unlost
for all frustration, to push his way beyond
whatever he is.

Madam, I'm . . .
    Look, ma! Look quick! I'm . . .

The sheep resumes
    its munching at the grass.

The Christoi*

With hankering for neither laurel nor halo,
his prayer directed to that God
who "need not even exist to reign,"
Baudelaire implored, "Grant me the strength
to do my duty immediately every day
and thus become a hero and a saint."

    Hero?   Saint?

Hero is apt to be preëmpted
for such as Achilles, Nelson, Guynemer, Frank Luke.

And *saint?*
Dominic who dearly loved a whiff
of sizzling flesh enhanced by screams?
Olaf the killer from ruthlessness and greed?
Raymond, Thomas à Becket? So many
who neither meant nor did well, at best
wasted their lives in empty rhetoric
and at worst . . .

Hero *and* saint. Prometheus, except for being
slightly more mythical perhaps than some.
A saint who hates the godhead?
(Knowing what would be Zeus's undoing,
he chose rather to have the vulture tear
his liver through the ages than to reveal it
to him and thus prolong gods' tyranny over man.)
The need is for a word to cover all
who try to scale the face of heaven, thieves of fire,
* See Glossary.

to bring back "secrets for changing life,"
every Prometheus, from the Aurignacian
who gouged mammoths in the cave of Arcy
to the man of Amsterdam who painted
the flayed ox carcass, from the one who first
pierced holes in reeds to him who died known mostly
as the sire of twenty children and highly skilled
performer on both organ and clavichord.
(The *great* Bach, most agreed
was Karl Philipp Emanuel.)

A term to fit Saint-Just, age 26 years two days,
standing on the scaffold in his master's blood,
and the boy choosing prison rather than be sent
to murder freedom-lovers half a world away.
Christos (from χρίειν, to anoint)
shall I say. Anointed, elect, chosen.
Chosen by whom?
Why, by themselves, I think.
Settle for christos, christoi.

Yes, *they* did the choosing. Chose once for all
and then again at every moment. Wisdom learned
at every choice making the next choice harder—
and easier!
Cézanne, the banker's son of Aix, along the road
to Le Tholonet, studying la Montagne Sainte-Victoire,
hours on end, day after day,
stopping to wash his brush after every stroke
to keep his mind a fresh blank for that choosing
less choice than discovery.

Proust—one book of a million-and-a-quarter words.
Every image, balancing of shape and sound, intonation,
every pattern of texture or construction,
every rhythm, color, tint, a choice—
a choice yet not a choice. ("... *we are not free*
before a work of art, we cannot fashion it
to our own wishes. But since it pre-exists us
and is both ineluctable and hidden,
we must discover it
as if it were a law of nature.") Every choice
a choosing (discovering) of self and selves
to *make* the choice. "*Un des moi* . . . *l'autre moi* . . .
le moi qui venait de renaître . . ." (Unless
ye be born again . . .)
The pampered little pederast chose nameless God
and, choosing God, chose agony and abnegation,
perpetual adoration.
Devoured by the cancer of holy Joy, the blessèd anguish . . .
"*cet appel vers une Joie supra-terrestre*"
(the *appel* itself is Joy). Consumed,
eaten away by "ineffable Joy . . ."

Péri, facing the firing squad at Mont-Valérien.

Some of them not entirely housebroken.
Pounded on the keyboard with a bootjack
to prove that it was out of tune. (He hadn't heard
a sound these many years.)
Broke his lease because his landlord tipped his hat to him.
His way of eating, particularly in his latter years,

was, shall we say (Grove does), "unbearable."
Spilled ink on the piano.
Shook the rain water from his hat all over
his host's furniture and books.

Maybe he is boasting when he tells of being a successful pimp.
For various reasons—*qui ne m'entent n'a suivy les
    bordeaulx*—
relatively few first-rate poets ever are.
He did, however, kill a priest, take part
in robberies and muggings. Let off from hanging,
"in view of the ill life of said Villon,"
was banished for ten years from Paris and its environs
and never heard of again.

Wiped his muddy boots on the new cretonne curtains.
Stood naked in the window, throwing his clothes
down into the street (because, as he,
country boy of seventeen and never been
in a bourgeois house before, dared not explain
to these belles dames de Paris,
they—the clothes—were crawling with lice
even before he left Charleville).

Some of them are indeed Titans
but I am struck by so many of them
being ordinary men differing from their neighbors
only by speaking out when others are keeping silent,
by saying "No" when others are giving dull assent,
by looking at situations clearly

and acting, within their means, accordingly,
by branding lies as lies.
What did he mean (this insurance executive) by
"The common man is the common hero?"

Caduceus

There
    in the meadow   lying on his belly
                          by the towpath
     grass   new and lush
           are
sprinkled   heels crossed above his back
    with pale
        at least
flowerets too frail and insignificant
     19 ways
              to have a name
   he thought
     of being
 Je EST un
     shat on
          autre
    by
  why not
   as many different
 Je SONT
     kinds of
         beaucoup d'autres?
    black birds

Il n'y avait donc pas de merles en Abyssinie?

Desnos

All bear witness,
some in a warped, obscure, circumvented way,
to human dignity . . .
> (Plenty there are
one wouldn't care to have around the house
of a rainy Sunday.)

"HERE lies buried an unknown chosen one
marked mostly
for his various ineptitudes.
That glow about his head, sometimes mistaken
for a halo,
was the buzzing contrail of the Furies."

A scale to judge them by? There is none.
To rate the strength of winds, intensity of earthquakes,
magnitude of stars, yes. To measure, balance, to count
the christoi, no.
"Who? *That* one! Look, I knew him when
he was ghosting papers for ladies' study clubs
and stealing hubcaps to keep himself in gin."

There have been fools and cowards among them—
touched for the moment—
and those who, having chosen,
went back on their choice.
Desnos, that slope-shouldered juggler-with-sounds
behind his bug-eyed lenses and with his tricky sleight—
I say that, once his life and words caught flame,
he stands among the christoi.

        At Compiègne
before they jammed the prisoners in
200 to a boxcar for a five-day journey
without water or food, the SS ordered
the Communists among them to step forward.
No reason he should do it but he did,
well knowing what it meant.
                        Buchenwald,
the blare and glare, slaps, kicks, curses in ten languages,
roll calls standing at attention half the night in rain,
beatings, starvation, the exhaustion of
shuffling corpses. "Out of all this
I want to make a song . . . an epic poem.
No, a cantata. It has the stuff of a cantata."
Through the month's forced flight—Auschwitz,
Floha, Flossenberg, Terezin,
under the thud of blackjacks and rifle butts,
he clutched the box that held his stub of pencil
and the unfaltering spate of poems.

Delivered by Czech guerrillas from the concentration camp of
Terezin, Robert Desnos died of typhus before he could be re-
patriated. The box in which he carried the poems that he had
written over the last sixteen months of his life was found by a
fellow *Häftling* who, seeing that it contained nothing but scrib-
bled scraps of paper, emptied it and used it to carry his own
scant belongings in. Citations from his poems published in clan-
destinity are engraved on the walls of the impressive Mémorial
de la Déportation, on the upstream end of the Ile de la Cité. The
only poem that his Czech friends salvaged was addressed to
Youki.

It sang in him
Poetry sang in him
Love sang in him
Love and Liberty and love of Liberty
His liberty   your liberty   my liberty
sang in him
and let him die all poet and hero and all saint.
       ("Convertir la haine en espoir.")
His words live on the granite walls
of the staunch, anguished prow that cleaves the Seine:
CAR CES COEURS QUI HAISSAIENT LA GUERRE
BATTAIENT POUR LA LIBERTE AU RYTHME MEME
DES SAISONS ET DES MAREES DU JOUR ET DE LA
                                        NUIT

I wish that those whose deadly smirks mock all
that such men live for
could read it as it stands there, read it
with their eyes and lips and jelly in their bones.
They would not believe it, but there *are*
"hearts that hate war and beat for Liberty."
Crush them in the most savage ways you can devise
and they will still outlive you.
These hearts that "beat for Liberty
to the very rhythm of the seasons and the tides
of day and night" can not be stilled.

Great? Only as thousands like him were.
No stuff there of a solar myth. He was
a boy grown to be a man who did not shrink
from suffering and dying for what he loved.

And, being human, would not allow being made
a walking carrion to diminish his humanity.

Gabriel Péri who died "pour des lendemains
qui chantent." (O doux Jésus! That sing at Ben-Suc?
My-Lai?) No morrow within the span of any now
on earth will ever sing again. All you
who died in *hope* were dupes, though none the less
christoi.
　　　　Christos, Van Gogh with his 39 crows
above the wheatfield on the road to the cemetery
of Auvers. Great, absurd Balzac.
Wolfgang Amadeus Mozart, whose letter to
his cousin Anna Maria Thekla read in part:
"Dreck!—dreck! . . . o süsse wort! auch schön
o charmante! . . . dreck, schmeck und leck!"
and more of the same,
which is regrettable but didn't keep him from composing
the Quintet in G Minor—nor Flaubert from saying that
"the three most beautiful things God ever made
are *Don Giovanni*, *Hamlet* and the sea."
The hand that carved in mammoth-tusk the Venus of
　　Lespugue,
the parturating virgin mother of God . . .
I looked at Alberto Giacometti and saw
the furrowed, Gauloise-smoking monkey face
of one of the christoi.

　　　　Christoi all
those whose little donkey-rides
are preludes to Golgothas.

And It Came to Pass

. . . Not so much an anagogic urge
as an impious itch to change
himself, his world, his universe,
without the slightest certainty of bettering them . . .

> *Choice between*
> *pitying and admiring the poor brute*
> *we cannot blame*
> *for being caught inexorably in*
> *a process of evolution that has not abated*
> *since first a set of gills*
> *was turned in on a pair of lungs—*
> *has, on the contrary, acquired more and more momentum.*

"Our modern world," Teilhard points out, "has come about
in less than 10,000 years. And in the last
200 years it has changed faster
than in the course of all the preceding millenniums."
He wrote that back in 1941 when there were still
choo-choo cars and atoms were unsplit
and forcing young men to baste babes in napalm
from safe distances would have been considered in bad taste,
the farthest man had ever been from earth was 10.6 miles,
and nobody had set eye on the backside of the moon.

And it came to pass that the Lord God spoke out of the
     mouth
of a Kansas preacher and said unto Luther Burbank,
"If I had meant there to be pitless prunes,
white blackberries, spineless cactus and blue poppies
I would damn well have made them that way."

Now in those days Luther Burbank had confessed
in an unguarded moment that he was not too sure
there really was a God—not that he was an atheist,
just didn't know for sure.
So the Lord God, or so the preacher said,
up and struck him dead to prove He did exist,
the old man being three-score and seventeen.

Burbank was a simple, kindly, unambitious soul
with no yen to get fame or profit out of his "creations,"
as he termed them.
He was not a scientist, had little education,
did not know
an isotope from a neutron
somehow he never even got an honorary degree.
He knew some aspects of nature from having spent
a lifetime puttering around to see what happened.
One would have thought he was the sort of man
God would have liked.
But according to His mouthpiece, No.

"Wizard of Plants!" the obituaries screamed.
"Never in all the history of horticulture . . .
Eight-hundred-odd creations . . . The mind reels
to think . . . One of the greatest
benefactors . . ."

The facts . . . Well, he did develop and name
the Shasta Daisy—"handsome in borders . . .
soon dies out . . . best grown as a biennial."

Most of the other things—pitless prunes, plumcots,
white blackberries—seem not to have caught on,
though, where it has not reverted, jackrabbits
will eat spineless cactus for want of other food.

Good Friday

Hosanna! Hallelujah!
They threw down palm branches all along the way.
(What the owners of the trees and of
the borrowed donkey thought remains unstated.)
Today is Sunday. Four more days to go.
They threw down palm branches. (Who is *they?*
And where were Francis Cardinal Caiaphas
while this was going on, and Pontius X. Pilate?)
    They threw down palm branches, and the donkey
("What was the slipperiest day they ever was?")
gravely setting one neat hoof before another
walked on them.
    I am trying to see the man's face.
    The answer is there, there and in what
he is doing with his hands.
    Waving acknowledgment of cheers? Uplifted
in benediction. Raised in a V sign or triumphant
clenched fist? ("The winnuh and still
      champeen . . .")
I cannot see the face.

Descended into hell.
    ("What's slipperest day they ever was?" Tommy, the
     Slovak
spittoon-emptier on the nightshift, used to ask
regularly twice a night. A crafty glint.
"Day Christ go through Jerusalem on his ass. Huh!
Got yuh that time." His only joke in English.
He treasured it until I explained and spoiled it for him.
"Donkey? What's is 'donkey'?" Four legs, long ears,
hee-haw, hee-haw.

In Slovak the word was *vosel*, he said, and looked
   nonplussed.
"Why Christ he's ride a *vosel*—rich guy like him?")

Descended into hell on his ass
and not even his own
Descended into hell through a flurry of ticker tape
Descended into hell   into hell

The Surf

WHITE NOISE
environs me and bears me up and out
    The Lord is obviously no shepherd of mine
The swirl of
WHITE NOISE . . . surf . . . a grain of sand . . .
    At Finisterre in equinoxial storms
breakers will scoop up pebbles and strew
them over the cliff and into parish closes.
Veils of spray sweep miles inland.
Sheep huddle in the fog,
lost together.

This is the fourth day   and no coming forth . . .
    Lazarus, you remember meeting me in hell?
Marsyas, the name is.
"No, I cannot say I do."
    I remember   I remember
I remember only the white
surf roar and the dank spume
of loneliness.
         Lazarus, do you remember me?
Shadow among shadows, faceless dream
   groping among dreams,
shade circulating among shades
tapping out their ways with white canes.
Midnight. It has always been midnight. Tomorrow is
midnight.
         Lazarus, don't you remember me?
Marsyas. I am the fellow inmate who whispered to you,
"Today is midnight."
         And the great horologe

boomed forth the twelfth stroke.
    (Actually it was
    another grain of sand
    trickling in the hourglass.
    This has long been going on,
    the deafening crump
    of a grain of sand trickling in the hourglass.)

My name is . . . My name is . . . hmm . . .
You! You that were resurrected! Do you remember
what I said my name was?   My name is . . .
Adam   Icarus   Marsyas   Ishmael   Merlin

Mélusine, from this dank, jumbled death-bin,
I cry out to you   knowing well
no answer ever will come. (Look goddamn it,
you can write. You know the alphabet, you have hands,
a sheet of paper, pens, pencils, a typewriter.
You have written books. Or don't write. Sign your name.
Or make an X—Mélusine, her sign.)

Black Squirrels and Albert Einstein

Questioned as to the chiefest goal of science,
he sniffed, "To keep the scientist amused."

. . . Communicated little those last years
even with his colleagues. Shunned underwear and haircuts—
and socks, because they only led to holes.
And who needs cuffs? He lopped them off to save on laundry.
No paper handy, he would lie abed
and scribble equations on the sheets.

　　"The two-three times you might say we got chatty,
　　all he talked about was squirrels—how ours
　　in Mercer Street aren't like the ones in the old country.
　　Kept repeating. Genius maybe, but he said
　　almost the same things every time we talked."

What *is* there you can say to strangers,
to the perennial strangers who live next door
and you see every day?
　　　　　　　　"Nice weather"?
　　　　　　　　　　　　　　　"Hot enough
for you?"
　　　　　　　　"Who do you pick to take the series?"
Or what's wrong with repeating? There are those
who love it. Homer, for all his "strong-greaved Achaians,"
"Hector of the shiny helmet," "Apollo of
the silver bow," still holds his own in paperbacks.
　　　　　　　　　　　　Or take the case
of Mado, wondrous little whore girl, sweet
presence tinged with shades of Jules Pascin—
and loved her work. (Nothing is—unquote—

work unless you'd rather be doing something else.
Which never happened to her.) Still,
as the song asserts, "they don't make jam all night."
Man is a talking animal. But talk of what?
I tried bicycle races: she had never seen one.
Love: it was too much like talking shop.
Books: she had never read one.
Food: she was no gourmet. Clothes: she spent
her more meaningful moments not wearing any.
I lit on history—Louis Quatorze, at random.
He struck a spark. Louis Quatorze liberating
Brittany. (She came from Plougastel.)
Louis XIV and la petite O'Murphy.
Louis XIV and the retreat from Moscow.
Louis XIV and the rape of the Sabines.
Louis XIV and, oh! that Christmas night
crossing the rivière de la Loire to take
the drunken Hessians—des espèces de boches—
in the rear! Combining, as it did,
Christmas and boating, it was, next to
Louis XIV letting the old woman's cakes burn,
her favorite story. Encore! Encore!
and never change a word. Allons, encore.
    "Et le bon Roi lui dit, 'Bien merci, Mademoiselle
                              Pocahontas.
Tu m'as sauvé de la mort et du scalping.
Je te fais donc Comtesse du Barry . . .' "
    "*Duchesse* du Barry! Tu vois que je ne dormais pas.
I only closed my eyes to listen better.
Encore. The one about the time he shot
the apple off the little Prince's head."

"All he could talk about was squirrels. No kiddin'—
black squirrels with tufted ears!
Seems in the old country that's how they come."

Yorick

"Nice guys finish last"
Leo Durocher

And those who only floundered, flapped
like oil-sludged gooneys and never did
get wing-borne?

Call him—I knew him well—Yorick, A. P. Yorick.
Slow-spoken, gentle, patient, a good mind,
face of El Greco's *San Luis Rey de Francia.*
"I think that I know how to see. I have
métier, almost as much as any living painter that I know.
Not that that means much. I work hard and every day.
Yet somehow what comes out is not *my* painting—
only a sort of exercise I learned that never quite came true."
Each picture *started* fresh enough. He primed
and stretched his own canvases,
best Belgian linen, Foinet hand-ground paints
(even for sketches, she wouldn't let him skimp).
She sat there in the atelier, knitting, reading,
sometimes herself painting in watercolor, always taking care
not to let her being there disturb him.
She loved to watch him paint—his quiet dedication,
sure touch, taste. That was all she asked
for having had the privilege to give
the funds that left him free to be creative.
Never, although she too had studied at the Slade
before their marriage, did she comment on his work
except to tell him *that* day's work was good . . .
as it often was in the first stages,
before it faltered and went limp and died.

The finished, stifled canvases stacked deep.
Desperate one day, he asked Paul Burlin for advice.

Burlin, who at that time was painting
lopsided incandescent cows erupting
into explosive heavens and convolute siestas
of coveys of lady acrobats,
because he saw and liked them that way,
stood for a moment teetering on his heels
before the latest work, a big one, some
eight feet by six, of three competently done
hieratic nudes. He studied them.
"What are they? Muses? Graces? Fates?"
Just women, Yorick told him. Burlin shrugged.
"Well, maybe they're okay, except they seem to come
from a world where no one ever got a hard-on."
A word that Mrs. Yorick didn't know. When he had left,
she asked what Mr. B. had meant.
And Yorick stammered, "Well, I suppose you'd say
he found them rather parthenogenetic."
She did know what *that* meant and thought it was
the nicest compliment she'd ever heard—
would never have thought that Mr. B., whom up to then
she never quite had liked,
could have such sensitivity.

　　　Read Freud, Jung, Adler. Learning that Otto Rank
lived in Paris, signed up to take a quickie
in ten sessions. One day halfway through,
professed finding his faith begin to wane.
"For instance, what's to keep me from *inventing*
dreams to tell him? Say, something so absurd
no one could dream it—like that I owned
a white elephant that followed me everywhere

I went . . . couldn't get rid of her because
I couldn't bear to hurt her feelings?"
Why not try it on him? I asked. "You mean it?
He wouldn't see that I was spoofing?
Well, I suppose I might."
Next time we met I asked if he had told
the analyst his dream. "What dream? Oh, that.
No. When I tried to I found it was so crazy
I couldn't even remember what it was about."

       . . . Ascetic . . . Ate and drank sparingly.
At table sketched to keep his hand in.
. . . and studious . . . austères études . . .
      Uccello's composition
      Degas's rendering of volume as in the
             yawning laundress's belly
      Manet's brushwork,
      the frescos of Tavant
      Gislebertus of Autun
      Hiroshige
always coming back to Rembrandt, Cézanne, Georges de La
   Tour,
Michelangelo, Piero della Francesca. Even learning much
from painters he didn't care much for:
David, Constable, Pascin's erotic line.
Going through Montauban, he stopped off for a week
to study Ingres.

Stillborn canvases stacked against the walls,
ready to be turned face-out and shown
if ever anybody cared to see them.

Seven viae dolorosae to the week
and every night Gethsemane. She would beam,
"From the very first,
my faith in him has never faltered.
His day will come."

Burlin—he was knocking off awards
and selling canvases as fast as he could cover them—
took pity on him.
"Jesus, hombre, I'd quit
painting if I didn't get any more fun out of it than you do.
There's a million ways to make a better living easier."
Yorick's lean El Greco face went instant white.

Yorick a christos? Who's to say?

Masque for Luis Buñuel

Director of *Viridiana* (1961), *The
Exterminating Angel* (1962), *Belle de
Jour* (1968), *The Milky Way* (1969), etc.

1

Pan in priest's livery or archpriest in Pan's.
Cleft hooves are castanets and, rictus in reverse,
even his bluntest jokes will have their subtleties,
impelling voyageurs to slip behind
the heroic statue on the esplanade
of the City's twin titulary goddesses
and, stifling for the instant tears and prayers alike
for the drear living and the luminous dead,
masturbate against the KEEP OFF THE GRASS sign.

2

The realm he reigns in   hopelessly abounds
in answers deftly shorn of questions
Incongruous clarities
unveil themselves at random—
lewd homilies   in flesh and bone,
precisely documented blasphemies.

3

In the strained silence of the blizzard night,
sole stir the blurred   traffic lights
blinking to one another, a mouse
nibbling at the wires set off the
burglar alarm in the delicatessen store
across the street. It rang all night
and well into the dawn
over the untracked, drifting snow.

4

A scream? Pay it no mind.

Tall in her naked ambiguity—
tapered flanks and groove of spine,
the stately callipygian wraith
poses before the pier glass
that gives back no reflection.

5
        Hah!
raped by her paternal uncle, rumor says?
Holà! She on the eve of entering holy orders
and he a high hidalgo famed for pious works!

6
A breath stirs the cold ashes on the hearth
of the deserted pavilion.
A Boule horologe, gilt and tortoiseshell,
grinds out the threadbare hour.
It is dawn because a heavy two-wheeled dray
rumbles over dewy cobblestones
to plop of fetlocked hooves.

7
And autumn.
        In Aragon a bandy-leggèd priest,
followed by *vendimiadores*, their baskets slung
across their shoulders,
stumps forth to bless the mountain vineyards.
        ¿Y usted, don Luis, qué tal?

8
    Qué tal, indeed!
O maudlin Minotaur, Proteus, profound,
translucent troglodyte!

    9
His devious sobriety provokes silent catcalls,
sniffs, lubricious intentnesses   And look!
down all the aisles, through all the exits,
trampling the usherettes who would restrain them,
people are walking out
                    Too late

    10
the harm is done.   A gong tolls. Enter the Angel
    of the Lord herding across the banquet hall a flock
    of rams and ewes in heat. Jammed between the
        porphyry posts and banisters of the monumental
            staircase, they flounder upward, the ewes half
                trampled, half mounted, by the rams. Their
                    bleats become more frantic, then dwindle. The
                    guests, more famished by the moment, lick
                        their chops and exchange knowing glances.

                        "Simon, son of John, lovest thou me?"
                        "Aye aye, Lord."
                        "Feed my sheep."
                        "Yassir. To whom, Lord?"

The Angel appears at the top of the staircase. He brandishes
    his flaming sword and triumphantly exhibits a dripping
    ram's head. Horns blare.

The spotlight fades to a faint glow. A sudden squall of snow
   hides the Angel. When it abates, he is seen wearing the
   ram's head and holding his own haloed head aloft in
   his hand.
The lights go out. A screen shows a slide of Whistler's
   Mother. Gradually she takes on dimension and assumes
   the profile of the ram. She sits motionless for several
   seconds, yawns widely and loudly.
One after another the guests, now replete, belch, yawn and
   fall asleep leaning on each others' shoulders.

11

On a Guinea beach a covey of small cannibals
utters shrill cries and scatters in all directions
before a troop of Franciscan missionaries who,
with loud halloos, their robes tucked up to their knees,
pursue them with gilded bows and arrows, shouting
"Praised be the Lord!" every time
they transfix one to the sand.

12

Good Friday, church bells silent for the day
good Judas will give sway to his good remorse.
The Good Samaritan will lend a length of rope
measured for drop and weight, suggest the tree,
recoup the cost by selling snippets of
hanged-man's lucky noose, more efficacious
than mandrake, four-leafed clover, rabbit's foot.

13
[*Pianissimo*]
To the cadence of martial music

ghosts of the sheep, now resurrected as goats,
parade through the banquet hall, bearing
banners, eagles, croziers. A tuba and a glockenspiel play:
    "Rock-a-bye, baby,
    On a tree top.
    When the bough breaks
    The cradle will drop
    [*How these lines run*
    I do not recall]
    Down will come baby,
    Cradle and all."
[*Fortissimo*]
    DON LUIS!
          [*diminuendo*]
              Don Luis!
                  [*piano*]
                  don Luis . . .
Several seconds pass before a faint echo says:
    Don Luis Buñuel.

14

He has released a statement to the effect
that this must be the last film he will make,
explaining that he is now too confirmed an alcoholic
to render the murky radiance of
his hallucinatory world.

The Dutch Head Nurse

In the American Hospital of Paris
where three of the doctors and two nurses
        were American,
the happy young Lapland nurse explained,
"Is okay my coontry only is too much cold
and winters is no sun. Is good only for reindeers."

She was no reindeer   rather a bright-eyed
flicker-tailed ibex or chamois
with nimble thighs that only fear of seeming senile
kept me from stroking.
She was tinkering with my transfusion apparatus,
business of trying to make the blood drip faster
but mostly an excuse to babble
in her freshly improvised English,
when another nurse,
squat, middle-aged and fire-breathing,
scuttled in. "What are you doing here!
You have not the right. Only I
may touch these things!" and shooed her from the room.
No sooner gone than the Lapp girl slipped back
"That one is hade noorse. Is Dotch."
She made it rhyme with Scotch, it sounded like a malediction.
"She is not liking me. I am not knowing why.
I am kind and gentle, good.
I am liking all peoples,
but that one, no, she is not liking me.
Truly, I am not knowing why."

And the Veil of the Temple Was Rent

"Nothing I have ever done . . .
   Nothing I have ever done . . .
      Nothing I have ever done . . .
                  was

worth the
       {
        paper it was written on
        canvas it was painted on
        clay it was modeled in
        staves it was scored on
        etc.

"Nothing," he said, "thank God, that I have ever done
will last."
        Wrong:
a child cannot drop its rattle from its cradle
without the effect [unquote] being felt
to the outermost fringes of the universe.
True, the infant's name, if that is what you mean,
will not go down in history, nor the effect
necessarily be beneficial—
except as picking up rattles
is good for adults' waistlines.

"Nothing I have ever done
    ELI   ELI
      Nothing I have ever done
        LAMA
          Nothing I ever did
            SABACHTHANI
              was worth the doing."

By the Watch

10:12 a.m. /
I have my watch back. Apparently assured
that I won't swallow it. A busy leisure hour
when mops push lint from under beds.

I am speaking to myself of meaning,
of acts or thoughts merged with or divorced from
each other and words. "Mere symbols." The more mere
they are, the more final, deadly. Symbols . . .
the said thing or even the babbled or unuttered thing
is as committed as the done, or worse.
I am speaking wordlessly of meaning
in its relation to being said.
                        Meaning: //
the more you are resigned to letting it
come and remain unintelligible,
though not necessarily for want of words,
the more it twists, contorts itself, to *mean*— /
sharply, hardly, cruelly at times
(as if all meaning were not cruel in the end!)

Happening to have a hoe in hand
hilling the asparagus, I killed a snake once, /
a new snake, moving out of the stand
of buckwheat into a newfound world, venturing, /
gliding in innocent expectation.
I struck and immediately hoped that it was only grazed.
I could not bring myself mercifully—
mercifully—to take another chop
and kill it. Where is the life of a snake anyway? /
In the head that cannot close its lidless eyes?

in its length, already severed, that does its best
to stay alive?//
("Don't never die till sundown.") Come quickly, sundown.
Come quickly. I will stand beside it,
trying, by covering it with warm dust
as one lays one's coat over a hurt child in shock,
to ease its going.

    "Don't you want your drink now?" No,
I am still working in the garden. (Come quickly sundown.)
    "Aren't you ready to have dinner yet?" No,
I still have things to do.
                 "Can't you sleep?"
No/(this unspoken), this day I hurt to death
a young adventuring snake. The spring
is spoiled for me, the summer, the garden
that was to have been beautiful, the year
and years to come.
It was a young handsome thing of grace, /
exploring with its flickering tongue the world
it was to live in. If I could be a moment Christ, /
my single miracle would heal and resurrect it,
make it forget the anguish that came to it
this day and let it glide once more
out of the buckwheat toward the hollyhocks.

Nothing can forgive me.

Oh, I presumably have killed men, young men perhaps
as handsome as this snake was. I never saw them
through their goggles and windshields close enough to know.

But they were closing in to do their killing too./
Death was a way that they and I had chosen. /
Presumably they knew the world they lived in
and what further to expect of it. On the whole,
they got off luckier than I did— //
luckier than I did, as they could never know.

Woke each morning expecting to be dead
by nightfall, not too much concerned about it.
   "Man, this here airman's feeling/
pretty trepid./No special hunch or anything— /
just feeling trepid."
            tremble

Death with Pants On

"Ace of aces." I saw him once in Harry's Bar
("Tell the taxi Sank Roo Doe Noo")
standing there with an untouched glass before him.
Georges Guynemer, the name had come to stand
beside Jeanne d'Arc's and Roland's. Apart those eyes
and the palm leaves on the ribbon of his Croix de Guerre
reaching to his belt, looked no more godlike
than any other slight tubercular boy of 22.
Not at all the lightning-hurling Zeus
that La Fresnaye's heroic portrait makes him.

Never too sharp a pilot, often shot down,
his Spad riddled, himself eight times wounded.
"But, man, what eyes!" a fellow Cigogne told me.
"And nerve and—well, you've got to say, what luck!"
Two shots—tat-tat—two Fokkers down in flames.
Tat-tat-tat-tat! Tat-tat-tat! Tat-tat-tat-tat!
Eleven bullets: a Rumpler and two more Fokkers.
That night I saw him, his score was 48.
He got five more before his string ran out.

Monday, September 10, sick, irascible,
he had three Spads conk out on him,
force-landed them and met the omen with a tantrum.
Tuesday even his mechanic begged him
to give his crippled luck a chance to heal.
Bright oblivion culled him. His wing-man said,
"One moment he was there. The next the sky
was empty. Not a boche in sight. No flash!"
No trace of either his body or the Spad was found.

Fit apotheosis: the skies of France
his tomb and monument. Streets and schools
named for him, medals struck.

                        I think of others
Chapin, Sayre, Comygies, Nick Carter
whom I last saw spinning down in flames
toward La Chaussée. Their first fight—
if you can call it that. Unmatched for unreality:
as we straggled out of clouds into a well
of open sky, the red-nosed hornets swooped.
Most of us
never found a chance to fire a shot.
There were others. I forget their names.

. . . *For Approximately the Same Reason*
Why a Man Can't
Marry His Widow's Sister . . .

The first time I saw him was at Stella's,
rue Notre-Dame-des-Champs. Apple-cheeked manchild
right out of Satie's *Enfance de Pantagruel*.
Still married to Hadley. (Stella had just left Ford:
this party was to see if she herself
had any friends or if they all were Ford's.)

The last time I saw him was at
Robert Desnos' in the rue de Seine.
He wanted me to meet the ambulances at Le Havre
and smuggle them across the Pyrenees.
(I kept myself available, phoned every day;
nothing ever came of it.)

Youki was there as full and lovely
as a rowdy, randy Ceres. Legally still
married to Foujita, leopardskin-panted painter of
inscrutable nudes that looked like cats
and inscrutable cats that looked like nudes.
"Every time I go to bed with Desnos,
I think, 'Mon Dieu, if we should make a kid,
it would be a little Foujita—long-distance papa
him living in Japan.' Not that him give a damn, but still . . ."
Youki (christened Lucie) who had made history
of a kind in Tokyo by going as Eve
to a diplomatic *ballo in maschera*.

Desnos. Who ever would have thought that out of
word-play, sheer sleight of sound, Pan-piping—
"Mon crâne étoilé de nacre s'étiole—"
sure-footedness as prancing satyrs go,

would come that trumpet voice for blurred
purple dittos:
    "I listen and I hear you, Norse, Danes, Hollanders,
    Belgians, Czechs, Poles, Greeks, Luxemburgers,
    Albanians, Yugoslavs, all our comrades.
    I hear your voices and call out to you
    in a tongue that all men know—
    a tongue whose single word is LIBERTY."

Spoke, called out to Terrorists everywhere,
Terrorists with their home-made bombs that, like as not,
went off at the wrong times and places,
Terroristen who tossed stolen grenades into Soldatenheimen,
who jammed the frogs of railroad switches,
pulled spikes on trestles, found throats with
switchblade knives.
How effectual his message was
is anybody's guess. He died perhaps
the more the saint and hero for having few illusions.

    No handy way to burn a candle to him
    except perhaps to cross the street to Notre-Dame
    and Jeanne d'Arc's shrine. Not quite the same,
    though you can whisper, "A l'intention
    de Desnos et de Youki."

The last time I saw Youki she had been drunk for weeks,
bloated, a stranded whale aground
in Montparnasse where she had reigned
"la plus belle femme de France et de Navarre."

The next time I didn't see her
she was dead.

Berlin. Ernest—not Papa for some years to come—
up from Paris to see the six-day bike race.
Pauline was this time's wife. Dinner with Red Lewis.
A girl—Agatha?—prattled trilingually
of painters. Cézanne? Van Gogh? Picasso?
Juan Gris? Mais c'est à rire! Italians, yes.
But French, Spanish . . . Hemingway stood up and crashed
his fist down on the table. "El Greco is
        a cockeyed GOOD painter!"
The gnädige Fraulein squeaked and subsided mouselike.

        . . . can't marry his widow's sister . . .
12-gauge tranquilizer. At seven o'clock a Sunday morning . . .
having come through the night—and countless other nights.
How long had he been thinking of it? . . . "me a failed
Catholic" . . . thinking even in such terms
as how to pull the triggers?

        No longer apple-cheeked or cheeked at all.
        One WHITE silent bang where head had been.

And how to choose the day when there would be
nothing to be curious about?
        Whether Ordoñez would cut off the coleta,
            whether Anquetil would win the Tour de France again
            and get well hated for it.
        Whether the CIA would succeed
            in setting up a puppet state for Madame Nhu,

if and when and how any one
of a thousand events one can't help being curious about
would happen.

      Curiosity killed a cat. It did? How?
      What cat? Speak no ill of curiosity;
it has kept me living, lo, this many a year.

Minutes out of Naples for Algiers
the soup closed in. Too thick to see the wing-tips,
too high to buck above it. "Any chance,"
I asked, "of turning back?"
           "None that I'd care to take, sir—
what with Vesuvius and all."
He flew the deck so tight spume caked the windshield.
Then a sudden clearing, there it was—
dead ahead a waterspout, mean and hungry,
a sky-high, belly-dancing funnel. Velocity enough
to drive a copper rivet through armor plate.
Can you split-ass a war-weary C-46?
The British are good people to be scared with.
This young Limey set her on one wing
and yanked the yoke into his belly.
               (The answer is:
Yes, if you have to, but better not
have to more than once a lifetime.)

"God, this isn't praying. This is just to say
I'd hate to die before I learn
what happens to Mussolini."

(*What happened came some six months later.*
They strung his carcass up by the heels.
Not pretty but quite real. Nothing phony this time
Absolutely last appearance . . .
A pity though he couldn't have stuck around
"to get the beauty of it hot.")

Not Dawn Yet

Not dawn yet   or ever
though the silence is no longer white and blank
    and has somewhat abated
           (The square-bottomed nurse says,
               "Look, if those bars really bother you . . .
               We aren't supposed to
               but if I was just so busy I forgot . . .")
somewhat abated
    Nor is the protracted CUBE as absolute
      nor the click so irrevocable.

Think back,
   Now that the grass is rippled by the rain
and the disk of sun blurred by harbor haze
   Now that Daedalus has put aside his mourning
and the sheep gone back to mumbling its cud,
think back.

     ". . . rather have been sired by a dog-fox
       on a vixen or an alley tom on a good mouser . . ."

Would never have opted to be human?
A bootless speculation. Truths have a way
of not existing short of paradox.

To say that life is good would be to wring
all meaning from both words.
Renan with his "charmante promenade
qu'il m'a été donné d'accomplir à travers la réalité."
Yes, to Desnos too was given

a charming stroll to take—though through a
                          slightly different reality.
From Buchenwald to Floha to Terezin
is not too many kilometers as the crow flies,
but that was not their mode of travel.
The villagers protested at having all those corpses
strewn in the ditches along the way.

Death already on him when freedom came.
Temperature never less than 39.6 degrees.
Alena Tesarova, his Czech nurse,
brought him a wild rose blossom. The petals fell
at his first touch. He would not part with it,
kept it with him into his final coma.
Having this prickly twig a kindly fighting-girl
had given him was good. Having lived through
to liberty was good. Being a poet,
being a man was good.
Did that mean life was good? Had been? Is?
Allons, mon p'tit! Non, mais tu veux rire!
But being human, yes, at times . . . at times
when men are human.

No, I would not secede.
Not for all the Himmlers, Johnsons, Quislings,
Calvins, Torquemadas. I would not secede
even if I could be a grain of sand,
sovereign and absolute
(". . . a grain of sand is almost indestructible. It is the ultimate
product . . . the minute hard core of mineral that remains after

years of grinding and polishing . . . Even the blows of heavy surf
cannot cause one sand grain to rub against another.")

Choose rather
to be however distant
kin of the christoi, of their race,
sharing their vulnerabilities and servitudes,
privileged to owe reverence to such as
Beethoven, Sisley, Wm. Blake, Chardin, Giotto,
Dr. W. C. Williams of Rutherford, N.J.,
Villon, "povre mercerot de Renes," Arrigo
Beyle, Milanese, Domenico Theotocopuli,
Ravel—"Yes, a success no doubt"
(speaking of the *Bolero*) "though unfortunately
totally devoid of music." All of them . . .
Yes, the Yoricks, the gaunt, undaunted Yoricks.
All the race of blundering doers and undoers
of their destinies, the fumblers, the tanglers of their skeins,
the Masters, whose common anguishes we,
dazzled by their glories (invisible to them),
cannot see.

Arnaut Daniel (circa 1190)

Ieu sui Arnautz qu'amas l'aura
E chatz la lebre ab lo bou
E nadi contra suberna
Arnaut Daniel

My name is Marsyas. Everyone has heard
of how I challenged Apollo, my flute
against his harp. Midas, whom we had agreed on
as judge, gave *me* the prize. The Romans
put my statue in their forum, symbolizing
Liberty. My name is Marsyas. I bore away the prize
over Apollo, god of music.

Arnautz am I.
I reap the wind, ride an ox
to course the hare and swim against the torrent.

I am Marsyas. There is another version.
This time the Muses—his stable—were the judges.
When they gave *him* the prize,
he trussed me to a tree, flayed me alive.
Choose your own version. I am a crude,
goat-footed, flute-playing, wineskin-sucking
lout that would as soon
screw a Muse as look at her. Sooner maybe.
Depending how she looked.

I, Arnaut Daniel, was born at Ribérac.
I am one honest-to-God *good* poet.
Parchment is dear. Most monks are lunks.
Nobody else can read. What is there to do about it?
Niente. Absolutely *nada.* A couple of years from now
it will be spring again
and I shan't be around to see it.
Willows budding in the meadow, gentians,

jonquils in the woods, girls twittering
in patches of sunlight by the river,
giggling and squealing and hiking up their petticoats
thigh-high to wade ankle-deep trickles in the field,
and I not be there. I've had this cough since Sicily,
gone to make songs for Richard Lion-Heart.
Ten years from now nobody will have heard of me.
        Not only as a poet. *Shove poetry!*
One way or another, it has kept me eating
most of my life. But shove it all the same.
What I'll miss is girls stooping by the brook,
picking cowslips, raising their arms
to put them in their hair and show the sweet
profiles shaping out with spring.

Aï! given a few springs more and even the spawn
of my own loins won't ever have heard my name.
Their mammies will have told them,
"Your pappy was a travelin' man," or
"You are the offspring of a foreign dignitary
who, hearing of my beauty, sent his emissaries . . ."

Ieu sui Arnautz qu'amas l'aura.
Today a brown dog lay sleeping in the sun
outside the tavern. I said, "Hello, dog."
Without bothering to open his eyes,
he beat the warm dust with his tail.
I am Arnaut. I shall be planted in the ground before
that chestnut sapling first bears fruit.

        If you want to see
something of what my eyes have seen,

go down to Moissac's abbey—the twenty-four
Elders with their white robes and golden crowns
and burnished lutes and rebecs, the Christ in majesty,
the cloister. Moissac or Dalon or Cadouin
if they are still standing. Conques, Montsalvy.
Go down to Beaulieu in Dordogne;
the tympanum there shows the Last Judgment
with Jews lifting up their robes
to show the sign of their covenant with Jehovah.
I am Arnaut Daniel. I lived
in a not too unlovely world.

     Mr. Bodington, President of the
     British Chamber of Commerce of Paris and
     authority on Romanesque architecture of
     central, south and western France, said,
     "Browning was not a gentleman. I am surprised
     you should have read him."
     Questioned, he explained, "Why, the fellow was—
     uh, no need to cite specific
     instances—uh, vulgar, so to speak."
       (Something I must have missed.)

Anabasis

1

And the more he rode, the farther he went;
that was a peculiarity of his.
People spoke of him respectfully
and wondered why.
Sycophants laid his wife while he was out
transplanting geraniums. And wondered why.
Foundations awarded him grants and wondered why.
For a while, he too wondered why and then
gave up wondering and decided
either that it was very natural,
seeing that that seemed to be the way things were,
or that he and they and everybody else that counted
were crazy—which seemed to be perfectly natural too,
although he wondered why.

The conductor came lurching down the aisle and said,
"Say, don't I seem to remember seeing you somewhere,
ol' sport?" and wondered why.
He himself wondered where he was going and why.
With age, wisdom grew upon him:
he merely wondered why he wondered why.

2

                This
Puerto Rican kid sat on the front stoop
and ran his fingers across the strings
of the guitar his older brother was in jail for stealing.
After a while he sort of got the hang of it
and it sounded pretty good to him.
There were people going by in the street.

He wondered if any of them would hear it and remember.
Pretty good considering that he didn't know how
to tune it, had never tried to play
any instrument before and had no ear for music anyway—
which didn't make for too much to remember.

Ismael? Soy Marsyas, tu hermano de sangre.
¿Te acuerdas de mí?

(¿Melusina, te acuerdas de mí?)

Apocalypse

All precautions have been taken:
lampposts have been strung with garlands,
wreaths hung about the necks of statues,
certain graffiti that have of late appeared
on the walls of public buildings been effaced
and plainclothesmen posted to apprehend
their skulking perpetrators.
As a temporary measure for her own security,
Cassandra, put under adequate sedation,
has been allowed to repose her vision
in a comfortable subterranean retreat with padded walls.
The city fathers wear happy smiles even when shaving.
The priests cannot recall a time when the auguries
have been so favorable. Poverty, anxiety, fear
are soon to become obsolescent words.
Plans have been drawn up for a municipal festival,
field day, barbecue and Old Timers' Day in one,
with men's and women's barrel-rolling contests on the pond
and potato- and three-legged races with special prizes
for senior citizens of both sexes and toddlers under four.
Miss Meeker's Antiquity Shop is going to provide
an old-fashion hurdy-gurdy and Reverend Stythe
is going to disguise himself in a monkey suit and pass the cup.
The weather man has promised to coöperate.

Yet even in this atmosphere of merriment and thanksgiving,
we should be less than candid did we not confess
to having played doubly safe, taken precautions
against all possible eventualities.
We have—need we say more—propitiated

certain divinities, interceded with certain
ominous omens not to be sooth.

SCENE: *The Fair Grounds. The Mayor is standing on a plat-
form draped with bunting.*
"Friends, Neighbors, Fellow Citizens of this fair—
or should I say, *fun*-fair—city, I want to say
that this is the happiest and proudest day that we have known
since the ostracism of Aristides . . ." (*Approving boos.*)
Sounds of hurdy-gurdy, steam calliope, and
High School Marching Band. Cheers and wolf-calls as
Gerty Brukstis, who has already won the sack-race,
wins the junior strip tease by a split decision,
Reverend Stythe casting the deciding vote.
The only note of discord comes when it is discovered
that, to comply with safety regulations, the rifles
used in the clay-pipe shooting contest are firing blanks.
The antique motorcar event is won by
a souped-up, steam-driven Cugnot 1769
over a 1906 Stevens-Duryea.

GERTY BRUKSTIS, *as Little Red Riding Hood:*
"All right, buster. Just one though, and don't give me
                    mononucleosis."
THE WOLF, *whispering in her ear:*
"That's not all I'd like to give you, baby."

Titters, giggles, sniggers, squeaks and squeals.
        [*A siren*]
    WE INTERRUPT THIS PROGRAM TO ANNOUNCE
    THAT, AS OF RIGHT NOW, THINGS DON'T LOOK SO GOOD . . .

FLASH JUST IN FROM RHODES:
    COLOSSUS ON THE LOOSE!

Citizens turn to each other uncomprehendingly.
"What's it all mean? What's it all about?"
"You been following it?" "Roads? What roads?
I been saying all along that traffic . . ."

The High School Marching Band strikes up
"There'll Be a Hot Time in the Old Town Tonight."
MAYOR: "Stythe! Make 'em stop that goddam music!
Get everybody out of here!"

Mayor and Councilmen hurry offstage.

COLOSSUS WALKS   [COL
    COLOSSUS WALKS   [OS
        COLOSSUS WALKS   [SUS]

A bulk of silent thunder prowls the streets.
Walls reel on their foundations, towers sway.
It sweeps so low it scallops curbs
        and parapets of bridges.

Colossus walks. His brass feet clang on pavements.
His lungs roar, his breath flakes slates from roofs.
His brazen tufts of eyebrows twang.
His bronze enameled eyes see nothing before them.
His massive pubic mane is an untuned
deafening Æolian harp plucked by a whirlwind.
The brazen balls that ships were wont to pass beneath

clang doom at every stride.
The fluted folds
of an aurora borealis rustle in the black sky
behind his head and shoulders.

Let no man dare behold his face
nor any woman glance long at his loins.
Let no one frame a query in his mind.
Let no man hope: hope, overt or secret, is forbidden.
Let us smother babies in their cradles lest
their whimperings or coos distract him.
Do not cast flowers in his way: he does not care for flowers.
Nor palm leaves: he does not care for palms.
Only let our youths and girls—those carefully chosen,
those only without blemish—cast themselves
silently before Him, their prostrate bodies
carpet His way.

> (*Orders have gone out to throttle
> Cassandra in her cell this night.*)

BUT WAIT! HEAR THIS!
A miracle! although the Temple
and all the other idols were destroyed,
one statue, that of the Supreme
Vestal, though toppled from her shrine,
is scarcely chipped!

Let us decree a day of solemn prayer
to thank that Power who has vouchsafed this sign
to us in this our desperate hour of need.

COLOSSUS STRIDES. HIS INCANDESCENT SHADOW
TURNS CITIES INTO SMOKING RUBBLE.
FORESTS ARE ASHES. ONLY BONES
MARK THE COURSES OF DRIED RIVER BEDS.
THIS STATION IS SIGNING OFF FOR LACK OF ANY SURVIVORS.

From deep in the ruins of the city
a jukebox is playing:
  ". . . Praise Him all creatures here below.
  Praise him above, ye heavenly host . . ."
The needle is apparently stuck in the groove.
  "Praise Him above . . . above . . . above . . . "

A seething wind leaves lava bubbles in its wake.

The Brocken

Guess it to be night again because the stocky
Shetland-pony nurse is back and MR GOLDBLATT gone.
She takes blood-pressure. "Java goo' day?"
Lady, I had one—thank you—gawdawful day.
She has plugged her stethoscope into her ears
and heareth not.

"in the island that is called Patmos"

SCENE: A blasted—but *really* blasted—heath in the Harz
Mountains. Heaps of remains of what a short time back was
sophisticated weaponry lie about. Front center, an Army
Chaplain. He is obviously in a state of shock, delirious and
very drunk. His body is covered with more third-degree burns
than uniform. Other than this, he is doing very well. When
he had a face, it was probably a pleasant one. The blast
having vaporized all iron rations, he has been living for some
days on a diet of communion wine and wafers. He staggers,
waving a chalice. The thirst of his evaporation is agony. He
raises the chalice, gulps and sings:

> *"The mountaineers have hairy ears.*
> *They're hardy sons-of-bitches.*
> *They wipe their ass with broken glass*
> *And care not how it itches."*

He takes another gulp and addresses the non-audience:
"Oh, hi there, folks. I know you're out there somewhere
even if I can't see you. Might's well get to know each other.
Shouldn' wonder 'f we're the las' folks here on earth."
He gropes for his dog-tag and reads it by touch.

'Capt. Mephistopheles, U.S. Chaplain Corps.' That's right.
Joplin, Missouri. Spirit of denial.
Only I ain't denying nothin' anymore."

He drains the chalice and starts to sing again:
    "The mountaineers . . .
I'll say we're hardy, us mountaineers! Real hardy!
Bein' up here on this mountain . . . that and bein'
born and raised in the Ozarks . . . makes *me*
a mountaineer, I guess. Hardy! Live on maybe
for days yet. Lungs in cinders, burnt flesh
sloughin' off my bones. Can't breathe but still
can sing I guess you'd call it.
Hardy. Maybe live on for hours yet . . . or minutes."

He totters, sways, spreads wide his arms
to try to keep his balance.

A gigantic shadow, luminous and accompanied by
a rainbow nimbus,
cast on the cloud bank by the setting sun,
reflects his movements.*
Even after he drops dead,
the glow seems to linger on a moment
before slowly fading out.

* This phenomenon is known as a Brockengespenst (Specter of the
Brocken) for having been first observed on the Brocken in the Harz
Mountains in 1780.

The Red Virgin

Ceux qui savent tes vers mystérieux et doux,
Tes jours, tes nuits, tes soins, tes pleurs, donnés
à tous,
Ton oubli de toi-même à secourir les autres,
Ta parole semble aux flammes des apôtres . . .
Victor Hugo à Louise Michel, 1871

The portrait in the encyclopedia is kinder
than most. The black dress she always wore did not
exactly set her off. No, for all Verlaine's
ballade: "Louise Michel est très bien,"
she looks amazingly like our own Abe Lincoln—
The nose and forehead, the generous strong mouth.
Only her eyes, wide-set and deep, are beautiful.
What do you know of her except that a Métro station
bears her name and that she was called la vierge rouge?
Simple annal: born to a servant girl
by the master of the château (though some say by his son)
raised in the family, given a good education
she supplemented later with higher mathematics,
physics, chemistry, geology and such,
she qualified to be a teacher but refused
to take the loyalty oath. Heading a private
school, between her teaching and her charities,
she made time for politics and poems—among her best
an ode to our John Brown.

                  When Paris was surrendered
to the Prussians and besieged by Thiers—
Frenchmen fighting Frenchmen, she joined the defenders,
led attacks. (Under an artillery barrage,
she scaled a crumbling wall to save a cat.)
At the end—"we were seven at the barricade,
then three"—a rifle butt knocked her unconscious.
While her captors were busy looting houses,

she came to and walked away. Gave herself up
when the victors proposed to shoot her mother in her stead.

At the court-martial the charge was wearing a uniform,
bearing arms and using same, approving
the execution of two generals.
The prosecutor called for a death sentence.
Her clear voice rang out: "I will not
defend myself. I refuse to be defended.
Since it is clear that the one right allowed
to hearts that beat for liberty
is a slug of lead, I demand my share."

Presiding Judge: "I refuse to hear you further."

Louise: "That is all I have to say.
If you aren't cowards, you will kill me."

Deported to New Caledonia, half a world away,
four months on shipboard in a cage, she writes
not of the hardships but, like a child
on a first journey, of all the wonders:
the sea itself, fresh winds, the mighty storms—
later of the birds and animals, insects,
huge handsome spiders and curious plants.
She learns the Canaque language, teaches natives.

Back in France after nine years of exile,
once more takes up her battle for a world
with neither slaves nor masters.

Packed off to prison on the old complaint
the High Priest Caiaphas made to Pilate,
"He stirreth up the people," she accepted pardon
only "because in prison I am useless;
if they think their grace will muzzle me,
they're wrong." Wherever there were listeners
she spoke. She packed theatres. A bigot's bullet
in her skull was not enough to make her miss
her next engagement.
                In her spare time she wrote:
quantities of poetry, tracts, science fiction—
including a draft of 20,000 *Leagues under the Sea,*
which one day, needing money, she sold to Jules Verne
for a hundred francs—novels, plays—one
produced in London, memoirs, a history.

Oxford, Algiers, Amsterdam, Geneva, Glasgow.
Nearing 75, she was stoned in Brittany,
carried on the shoulders of workers in Poitou.

She died possessed of a few trinkets and piles
of manuscript. The procession following
her plain pine coffin took nine hours to pass.

People Walking

To *M. L. R.*

Here is a riddle: Here are people walking,
not to get to anywhere except, if their feet hold out,
back to where they started from.
Walking not for exercise or pleasure,
thousands of people most of whom have never seen
each other before today. Nobody is paying
or obliging them to walk. It makes no sense.

The rain is slackening to a drizzle.
Hour after hour, these men and women filing by
in quiet ranks. Some of them carrying
placards, banners, banderoles.
They spell each other off at holding up the staffs.
Many of them have walked in from distant suburbs
to walk here in the rain this afternoon
and then walk home again tonight.
Men and women. How many of them are there?
(*L'Humanité* will call them half a million:
Le Figaro estimates them at twenty thousand.)
Walking by twenty-odd abreast for hour on hour.

Many of them remember barricades
of café chairs and tables, overturned pushcarts,
cars, autobuses, garbage trucks. They brought out
their own bedsteads and sofas, hoping they would not
get too much smashed, and tossed their mattresses
down from windows. Mostly, their only arms
were what they got from Nazis they could kill.
To many of them, Auschwitz, Belsen, Neuengamme
are more than names. To some of them
Madrid, Terruel, Guadalajara, the retreat

across the Pyrenees, where they learned
all causes are lost causes, are fresh memories.

They are walking, not marching,
a Communist cell-leader beside a priest,
a world-known architect and critic keeping pace,
for all his eighty years, with lean Algerian laborers
and Vietnamese students. A two-star general
walks beside a woman in a blue work-smock.
In side streets along the way, detachments
of police with weighted capes and billies and gendarmes
with carbines stand by in case of trouble.
                                        No need.
When the walkers reach this point along the way,
section leaders turn and raise their arms;
all talk stops. I wonder why. A woman on the curb
calls out, "Bravo, mon général!" He puts a finger
to his lips, nods toward a sign I hadn't seen:
HÔPITAL: SILENCE. "Ah, pardon!"
she whispers. "Pardon, mon général."

The unmeasured tread of all these feet
has found itself a rhythm. My pulse beats to it.
I fall into the ranks. My voice joins
in the anthem the Red Virgin sang in prison.
A tall and very black Senegalese
hands me his pole to carry while he stops
to fix a broken shoelace. For the moment
I am an auxiliary of

* * * * * * * * * * * * * * * * * *
*   LES TRAVAILLEURS NOIRS DE BOULOGNE-BILLANCOURT   *
* * * * * * * * * * * * * * * * * *

When we arrive at the Place de la Bastille,
somebody makes a speech that no one hears.
Once more we sing the anthem:
> "C'est la lutte finale.
>   Groupons-nous et demain
>   L'Internationale
>   Sera le genre humain."

These are good people.
They want Vietnam to be free
and Algeria and Greece to be free
and France and America and every other country in the world
to be free. It is as simple as that.
They don't believe that walking in the rain
will *make* them free. But what else can they do?
This will say they *want* them to be free.

These are good people. They do not believe
what they are told to believe. They remember for themselves
what they have learned and known.
Living is not wasted on them.
They are good and brave people.
They have faith without hope
or hope without faith, or both without either.
They see no virtue in being gullible.

These are good people,
these people that I have walked with a little while.

These are brave people. As long as I am with them,
I too am brave and good.
These are innocent people. (There is no wisdom
short of innocence.)
While I am walking with them,
I too am innocent.

We are dispersing now.
The rain is setting in again.

I step into a doorway for shelter.
A woman says, "My dogs are killing me.
If I took my shoes off now, I'd never get into them again.
I can see myself walking from here to Saint-Denis
in stocking feet.
Mais on était beaucoup, hein! Dites donc!
How many would you say? Fifty—a hundred thousand?
Lots of us. It was really worth it."

Her job is punching tickets in the Métro;
her husband is a baker. That's why
he couldn't come today. He needs his sleep.
They have three kids that they are going to see
get decent educations.

"Visse, Scrisse, Amó."
Arrigo Beyle, Milanese

Me too. At random for the lives I lived.
Whose? Mostly good ones in any case.
At moments I have heard the opaque silence
that Giotto knew, the rock's reply to rock,
confirmed, made holy, by the sky. I have guessed
how wood and copper, china, felt to Chardin's touch,
have walked in quiet ranks with men and women
willing to die for what they knew
their dying could not save. At times I have seen
the freshness of the flood that morning
at Port-Marly through Sisley's eyes. I have waked
beside Valérie Marneffe, unlaced the stays
of Odette de Crécy. Pockets clanking with
"all sorts of arms and pistols," I have been
seduced up the ladder to her bed
by Mathilde de la Mole.
I have seen, death in my soul, the desperate beckoning
trees near Hudimesnil. I have breathed
Provençal noon through Vincent's nostrils.
       Vicariously?
No more than when a Sopwith disintegrated
at a thousand feet with me in part of it—shreds of memory:
avoiding names, pretending that I knew
everybody who seemed to know me. At mail calls,
none ever for me took figuring out.
"Who was your letter from?" "My folks."
(Everybody, even that ape Raz, it seemed,
had "folks." I asked him. A mother, sister, aunts,
he said. "Why? Did you think I was generated in a test tube?")
     No more vicarious
than whatever put those ribbons on my battle jacket.

No more than me, drop-out from night-school,
delivering the Honors Address at the Phi Beta Kappa banquet,
title, "Whosoever increaseth knowledge
increaseth sorrow," which the toastmaster cut down
to "The Purposes of Learning." Sometimes
running across a mention of
"this distinguished educator," I say,
"It seems to mean you, P.O.B."
It leaves him unimpressed. His greatest source
of lasting satisfaction: having contrived
to get a Paris street named for Saint-Just.

        Gamut of goddesses, tear-channeled cheeks
        and rough-hewn, yearning vulva of Rosmertha,
        mother, sister, mistress of the dead.
        Ishtar, Epona, I have drunk your milk and tears.

. . . cone of light in my eyes . . .
        All this is happening.
Lazarus, remember? I asked you for my name . . .
Thanks for refusing me an answer.

        Finis terrae . . .
Pen-Marc'h, horse's head.

. . . wandering among the stands of menhirs.
Some of them have eyes and concave cones
        to mark the breasts
cups and crosses
The drizzle has set in again   The dead move freely here.

I might speak to them   Gulls
and cormorants already answer.

   We have lived strangers' lives
   in depths and breadths of worlds they lived
   and died to make.

Lull in the gale.
Voices break as waves against a vaster
             finis terrae.
Boom of rumbling rocks hurled against the headland,
rattle of receding pebbles and water swirling—
race and undertow
gathering never-spent strength
to pound again   Spray falling in heavy curtains.
Boom of earth trembling with the shock
    felt a day's walk inland.
Sheep huddle in the fog.

        The dead are very near
      They move freely
          We talk together with no
      need of words

     The storm speaks.
It sings in me
    the litany of the christoi,
the named and unnamed, the forgotten, though not less
       close for that,
the unknown, the dead who are living
     their fullest lives now:

the man who set his feel of deer
        swimming a freshet
on the walls of Lascaux, he who somehow—
swimming, crawling, working his way vertically up
through darkness—came to paint the bison
in the caves of Niaux,
Louise Michel with her great spate of love—
and hate where hate was needed. Stendhal, "hussard
de la liberté." They who made
Falstaff and Charlus, Hulot, Pickwick.

Marsyas, do you remember me? Ishmael.

Strangers? Selves! Blood brothers.

"And the Evening and the Morning . . ."

(For some time a humming sound had been going on. It is augmented by the Voices mumbling to each other. By now it is so loud that Marsyas, who is standing in the middle of the stage in a hospital bathrobe, has given up trying to speak.)

A SHATTERING WHITE SILENCE BLINDS AND BLOCKS OUT EVERYTHING.

(Now the Voices and the masks they issued from
are gone. The young night nurse from the Intensive
Care Ward is sitting cross-leggèd on the floor to the
right of Marsyas. He doesn't notice her presence.
She is listening, though too tired, as she always
is at dawn, to try to understand what he is saying.
Marsyas is talking to the self that he has more or
less found.)

"I am called Marsyas and Merlin
I am called Ishmael and Icarus
My hide hangs on a thorn bush in Thessaly
The spells I taught her still imprison me
in a copse of the forest of Broceliande
Those are my limp lifeless legs that the sheep sees
       splashing into the harbor
Evenings at the water hole I lap with jackals
We snarl but make room for each other
We share our kill   Hagar before she died
taught me to make slings and harden
sharp sticks in fire
       [Shyly] I am also called Yorick."

Strange, the first several times I saw
Rembrandt's *Flayed Ox*, I somehow missed the girl
peeping in the doorway. I still can't guess
why she is there, though I am glad she is.
At Rampillon, if you look close enough,
on the gablet of a wall buttress you can make out
a fool in motley raising a stick to beat
a leashed ape. On the tympanum of a chapel in the fields
near Espalion, Hell and Heaven are switched around
from left to right, and the God presiding this reversed
Judgment Day is definitely horned, as horned
as any Minotaur. Frieze of the apse in that mountain village
where an old woman coming out of mass
and seeing me, a stranger, grabbed my arm and urged,
"Don't look at that, monsieur! Oh, no!
You mustn't look at that!" pointing, stabbing
her finger toward a basalt woman
grinning up from between sturdy legs
at her pronounced pudenda.
                              The queens of Chartres.
Blood-dripping fangs of Durga. Blessèd incongruities,
blends of majesty and bawdry, tenderness and horror—
and innocence.

(There in Mercer Street his thought ran thus: ". . . the
mysterious . . . the fundamental emotion that stands at the
cradle of true art and true science . . . The experience of
mystery . . . this knowledge and this emotion that consti-
tute true religiosity.")

The chiefest goal of science?
If he had said, "To grope toward God,"
they would have *known* that,
like all lovers of liberty, beauty, justice—
the man was crazy.

Judgment Day

"And—what is more significant—he [the votary]
calls himself by the very name of his god—he is
himself Bacchus."
Encyclopaedia Britannica, 14th edition,"Mystery"

The VOICES, *speaking through three huge terra-cotta masks*
that fill most of the backdrop:
  You who have passed through there lately,
  what was it like?
  Glutted vultures on dead branches of blighted trees?
  Labyrinthine gulch of milling blind and mad
  and all the seeing-eye dogs frothing with rabies
  and slashing at each other's throats?
  Corpses devouring the living piecemeal?
  No one able to reach and touch another
  except to carry pestilence or doom?

MARSYAS, *who is somewhat identified with Silenus, Bacchus:*
  Something of that. That perhaps is one way
  it may be seen.

The VOICES:
  One way? Perhaps? This from *you*
  who saw your bloody hide draped on a thorn bush?

MARSYAS (*He speaks casually, not trying to give a cogent*
  answer. He seems to be in a waking trance and communi-
  cating only with, groping for, himself.)
  Did dawn come? I suppose it must have.
  Did they give me back my flute and skin?
    No two grains of sand?
  The day I came to stand by Eucharis's tomb,
  Freya laid her arms about my neck
  And kissed me through our tears.

My name is Marsyas. I played a flute.
Forget that silly challenge. I played it best alone,
sitting on a rock or sprawled on banks of wolf's-foot,
checkerberries.
A chipmunk now and then would sit up and listen,
a rabbit froze, ears flat along its back,
after a while went on with nibbling.
A bluejay cocked its head and gave a squawk.
Once a box-turtle opened up and stretched
its wattled neck in my direction.
Nothing of an Orpheus about me. Not charmed,
only at length reassured that this beast with
its different kind of noise
was as harmless as a nickering horse.

The VOICES:
Enough maundering. Look, you left your hide there.
Tell us about the Harpies, the Erinyes,
Medea murdering her children. What about . . .

MARSYAS, *breaking in and speaking directly to the* VOICES:
Cruelties, stupidities, vileness a-plenty.
Filth, indignities, cowardice. What man
can say he never had a share in them?
Haloed lies gloated as they sniffed
burnt offering that we made them.
Brutalities claiming greed for their excuse.
Ishmael did well to take into his heart the cry:
"Woe to him who, in this world, courts not dishonor!"

(A *roar of bloodthirsty hymns accompanied by organ peals and
trumpets is heard in the distance.*)

"The Son of God goes forth to war
A kingly crown to gain.
His blood-red banners stream afar.
Who follows in his train?"

"Onward, Christian soldiers, marching as to war."

"Christian, up and smite them,
Counting gain but loss.
Smite them, Christ is with thee,
Soldier of the Cross."

                    Yet
there is innocence to be found there,
vast innocence of Einstein, Rembrandt, Blake,
Louise Michel, innocence that may be contagious,
innocence of the friend I have called Yorick.
Innocence of those who dare to take
strangers into their hearts and make known their love
with small tokens made, like as not, with their own hands.
Innocence of those who truly speak their minds—
        appalling innocence
of those who make no show of honoring idols
and recognize their God by the completeness
                        of His suffering.
Radiant innocence of the young man sitting beside
his young wife and talking of their chance
of going to prison for making known
their unwillingness to share in crime.

There is the innocence of the man no longer young
who dares speak sense to the mob of sly, malicious idiots
with stones and bottles clutched behind their backs,
who dares pit truths against their jibberish.

    ("*And when the battle's over, we shall wear a crown!*
    We shall wear a crown! we shall wear a crown!
    And when the battle's over . . .")

we shall be damn lucky if we still
are wearing heads.

Our God is innocent. He holds forth such awards
as only the very innocent could ever prize.

The Making of the Bear

Perhaps for fear of saying to oneself,
"Why you rather than another?" or asking
why it should be done at all,
it is not good to plan such things too long.

No question others had more craft than I.
I had waited for the Old One to give the sign
to one of us, half hoping still his choice
might fall on me. But lately he had turned
to graving stags and reindeer on bits of antler,
art that for all his pains my clumsy fingers
could never seem to master. In any case,
his choice for cavern walls ran to pregnant cows,
bison and ponies. That, and more and more
he favored places not too hard to get at.
"What's the harm in having good work seen?"

Meanwhile the first full moon of spring was near.

I can't say why I chose the cave I did.
Passing that way one day, I'd seen it
and taken it for a badger's hole until
I saw an owl rise from it and, listening close,
caught the voices of the water.
I set out before dawn and took along
well-scorched moss and tallow, stone lamp, firestick
in a deer bladder lashed tight with pitched sinews.
The flint I carried in a pouch tied to my wrist.
I crawled with hips and belly till I came
into a place where I could squat. There I made
my first light. The water sounded fairly near

though the first spur I took was full of twists
that led me further from it. I turned back.
Now inching on a ledge with steep sloped roof,
I struck a fissure where the torrent spouted.
I whispered to the spirit, filled my lungs
and plunged.
      Swim? I doubt a salmon could
have swum it. I braced and fought for holds
in walls and ceiling to haul myself along,
still with no sign that anything but more
and wilder water lay ahead, a chance
a man must take. Half-drowned, I reached a sweep
and lay there spewing out my lungs and caught between
terror of the dark and the solid feel
of rock beneath me. I hoped the bladder
still was staunch but dared not open it until
I knew my hands were dry. When at last I twirled
the firestick and coaxed the wick to flame,
I saw the place was far too open
to waste good work on.
      I edged my way along a slit so barred
by stone icicles that I would have given up
when, almost now in reach, I saw the wall
that I have known since childhood
yet never seen before. I saw it now
even to the scratches other men,
knowing the place for what it was, had made
ages before me. Some of their animals were not
like ours—one hairy beast with two horns on his snout
was half glazed over by a layer of stone-ice.
Many of them were drawn overlapping others—

as mine would sprawl on theirs. None of them
was anything the size that I intended.

The stone was even-grained, would take flint clean,
and yet not soft enough to flake with time.
Pressing my back against the other wall
to have full arm-room, I sketched him in—
a bear as big as living. I worked fast,
paused only when the need was to renew
the wick and tallow. First I got the spine—
that line where limberness and strength
of any living beast is—cut firmly,
the head scaled in and forelegs placed
before the tallow failed.
                         Spilling down the torrent,
then guided most by slithering in my own tracks,
I found my way out—into moonlight. The sun,
it seemed, had set twice since I left.
                    Ate and slept but, lest
the bear-feel be dimmed in me, did not go in
to either of my women.
I told no one where I had been nor why.

Next day I packed another bladder, taking
a good supply of moss and tallow, honey and nuts,
and other, heavier, newly beveled flints.
As a last thought, I went to see old Kill-Bear.
"Look like?" he puffed. "A bear? Why, you've seen bears
since you were a baby." (And drawn them too,
he might have said, since I could scratch earth
with a stick.) "Come now, you've seen those I killed.

Look like? Well, they've got hair all over them.
Stub tails, big paws and heads and lots of teeth."
I left the old fool bawling after me:
"Hey, you ain't found one, have you? You're supposed
to tell me if you have. Don't you go trying
to get my job by killing it yourself!"

I found the cave was easier going this time,
but the torrent sucked and swirled up to the ceiling.
I moved half into it to test its tug.
It grabbed me, pulled me under. The bladder buoying me,
I found a shallow dome that let my nose just clear
the water. Strange, there with death so sure, I thought
not for my women nor their young but for the bear
that I would leave unfinished. Him I commended
to the spirits of the dark.
                              Slowly the water
ebbed below my chin and then my shoulders.
It rose again and then as sudden fell.
                    I was on a rock shelf.
I had slept. The bladder was still with me.
The roar was gone, the water gurgled like a brook.

The new flints bit well. To give him weight,
I undergouged the belly and hind quarters.
A natural bulge I fashioned into head.
I gave him teeth and claws. Then last of all,
he took on eyes and nostrils. When he began to breathe,
I stopped and snuffed the wick, safe in his
protection, slept.
                    Waking and making light the last time,

I scratched a spear mark on his flank as we were taught—
so shallow though that he would never feel it,
made him an offering of honey, nuts and tallow,
ate some myself. The lamp and flints I left there.

Heft, strength, the saddle and the soles,
the rambling appetite, fur, the rolling amble,
the curious, investigating "Whoof!"
the clatter of unretracting claws, the bear-play—
sliding on their rumps down clay banks into puddles,
standing erect and balancing vines across their noses—
patience to wait with poised paw
                on a rock among the rapids
to snatch the salmon as they leap,
the good
bear-smell of being bears
            are what I had tried to make the flint say
            on the cavern wall.

            Ferocity and gentleness . . .

Your bear is one great fool and so is man!
I have seen a naked child in pigtails,
squealing her delight,
chase a full-grown bear splashing across the meadow—
and a half-grown cub stand up and brave
a dozen hunters with javelins and torches.

    Bison are better eating
    and their hides tan easier
    but you can't laugh at a bison.

Beside the profound, absolute
dark of caves, our night seems noon.
Even beneath a starless sky,
the eye makes out bulk and shapes,
but in winding scapes of underground
where no sun's light has ever shone,
finger may touch the lash
of open eye unseen.

           There
in that total lack of light
is where my bear is.
No one will ever see him
but he still
is there.

High Abyss

". . . où flottaison blème
Et ravie, un noyé pensif parfois descend."
Rimbaud

File in stiffly from the wing, bow to the audience
they make believe isn't there, spread tails,
take seats, set to tuning, open scores:
    STRING QUARTET IN C♯ MINOR
       Opus 131
The lumpy, bald one with the goldfish lips
    raises his bow.

        Flotsam,
         noyé ravi,
I have been an instant-lifespan borne,
flashflooded, up into an abyss,
caught by shrill serene tumult
    into cyclone depths beyond me,
effaced by vision more intense
than I could ever know,
lulled by a wild accord of warring energies.

       Noyé pensif,
I have come back having grasped perhaps as much
as a lightning bug, clinging through a storm
to a leaf's underside,
might understand by fellow-feeling
of the lightning stroke that in a single blast
has ripped the elm trunk all its length.

Four sweating men are drawing horsehair
across squills of lamb gut and silver wire—
and give the resin credit too; it makes the squawk.

Delirious order
of the march of suns and comets.

In this expanse of tranquil ecstasy that made
"cold tears of anguish and terror
seep painfully through [Berlioz's] eyelids,"
if I say "prayer," I have blown the word
        for ever use again.
If I say "grief," what of the tremulous exultation,
the clamorous glee, triumphant resignation?

And what of the fifth movement,
the lusty, raucous dawn,
gross repetitions, pizzicati plucked on frayed nerves
redeemed only by the reveilles answering back and forth
over the waking town . . . babble of the marketplace?
                        Hate its relentless jangle until
you come, to your surprise, to love it?

And the desolate resolve that breaks in close upon it?
And the headlong order of the finale?

Four by now—the quartet counts seven movements with
no pause between and tailcoats are warm—
much sweat-sodden men
are sawing resined horsehair
against strips of lambs' intestines.

              Beyond . . .
"Beyond beauty," as Wagner said
Beyond analogy   Coherence beyond coherence
Locus beyond space-time continuum
                    (Paddy . . . Mim . . .)
Dawn beyond all limit of horizon.

Four men bow woodenly, file off the stage
taking their instruments, leaving the scores
on racks behind them.

Glossary

BROCELIANDE   In this vast forest of Brittany the young Vivian laid a spell on her elderly lover Merlin that was to keep him forever captive and visible only to herself.

VIOLLET-LE-DUC (1814–1879)   Architect who restored many medieval monuments of France. One of the chimeras, often miscalled "gargoyles," with which he decorated the towers of Notre-Dame is a favorite subject of postcards of Paris.

'TITER-MARSHER   German hand-grenade of W.W.I, shaped like a potato-masher.

CHRISTOS, CHRISTOI   Pronounced to rhyme respectively with "lees toss" and "lees toy."

PAUL BURLIN (1886–1969)   American painter living in Montparnasse during the 1920's.

ARNAUT DANIEL   One of the greatest of the troubadours (circa 1190). He was greatly admired by Dante and is said to have been a favorite poet of Richard Coeur-de-Lion.

HUDIMESNIL   The reference is to a mystic experience of the hero of Proust's novel. Not being able to interpret the message that this clump of trees seems to be trying to convey to him, he feels as heartbroken as if he had betrayed a dead friend or denied a god.